*McMaster Journal of Theology and Ministry*
ISSN 1481-0794
ISBN: 978-1-62564-556-2
Editor
Lois K. Dow

McMaster Divinity College

1280 Main Street West
Hamilton, Ontario, Canada L8S 4K1
email: mjtm@mcmaster.ca

*McMaster Journal of Theology and Ministry* is an electronic and print journal of McMaster Divinity College, in Hamilton, Ontario, Canada. It seeks to provide pastors, educators, and interested lay persons with the fruits of theological, biblical, and professional studies in an accessible form. It succeeds the Divinity College's former periodicals, the *Theological Bulletin*, *Theodolite*, and the *McMaster Journal of Theology*. Each volume covers an academic year (September to August). Reviews and articles are posted on the McMaster Divinity College website at:

http://www.mcmaster.ca/mjtm/

and beginning with Volume Nine (2007–2008), the volume is available in hard copy as well.

The *McMaster Journal of Theology and Ministry* is also available on the EBSCO database, and abstracts are included in Religious and Theological Abstracts (RTA).

Manuscripts, books for review, and communications should be addressed to the Editor through the email address on the journal website. Contributors are encouraged to use the style outlined in the Author Guide of Wipf and Stock, available at: http://wipfandstock.com.

All articles and book reviews are peer-reviewed for appropriate academic and professional standards.

Copies of the printed version can be ordered from Wipf and Stock Publishers in Eugene Oregon, USA, 97401, through their website, wipfandstock.com. Copies are also available through the McMaster Divinity College bookshop.

Content of the *McMaster Journal of Theology and Ministry* is copyright by McMaster Divinity College.

For more information about McMaster Divinity College, please visit the College's website at www.mcmasterdivinity.ca.

## Spiritual Formation, Evangelicals, and the Christian Year

Eugene A. Curry
Park Hill Baptist Church, Kansas City, MO, USA

### Our Appropriate Focus

Any talk of tools or strategies for spiritual formation (such as this article will shortly present) must be preceded by a fairly obvious question: if we are to be "formed" in some sense, what "form" are we to take? In other words, before the process of spiritual formation can really begin, one must first identify its ultimate goal. What, then, does genuine spiritual maturity look like? Of course, any process of spiritual formation among us as Christians must ultimately seek to engender Christlikeness—that is, any program of spiritual formation must find its footing, its foundation, in Jesus.

After all, Jesus spoke of the relationship that ought to obtain between himself and his disciples as analogous to that between a vine and its branches (John 15:4–5). Through this image Jesus meant to convey not simply the idea of some trivial connection, but of utter dependence, of a relationship that provides us with our "life blood," existentially speaking.[1] Indeed, Jesus promises that by "abiding" in him and allowing him to "abide" in us, not only do we come to know who he was and is, we will come to know who we are as well—we find our truest identity, becoming the sort people that God has intended us to be.[2]

To take another of Christ's teachings, in the Gospel according to Matthew, Jesus declares, "A disciple is not above his teacher, nor a slave above his master. It is enough for the disciple that he

---

1. Köstenberger, *Encountering John*, 161.
2. Borchert, "John," 1071.

become like his teacher, and the slave like his master" (Matt 10:24–25a).[3] Christ is undoubtedly the teacher and master in this passage, and thus the apothegm stands as a reminder that Christians (Jesus' disciples) are to aspire to become like Jesus himself.[4]

The Apostle Paul asserted this same sentiment in Eph 4:11–16 when he spoke of God's desire that the Christian community "grow up" into the maturity and likeness of Jesus—a process that would unite Christians both to Christ and to one another.[5] Thus, in the end, "spiritual formation is the process whereby the inmost being of the individual takes on the quality or character of Jesus himself."[6]

## *A Further Issue*

With the ultimate goal of spiritual formation clearly articulated, one may then move on to the question of method: How might one seek to impress upon a Christian the "quality and character of Jesus"? How might a community of faith seek to form that complete spiritual maturity within its members from a practical perspective? It is, after all, one thing to know one's intended destination and quite another thing to know how to reach it. So how might we approach our goal in this instance?

Once more, Jesus himself is our paradigm as Christians, and while that is most immediately true of his person, his practice deserves consideration as well. And in his own ministry, Jesus sought to encourage his followers on to Christlikeness—that deep connection with and emulation of his own self—in a rather direct and obvious fashion. As the recently deceased Michael Spencer noted,

> Jesus made disciples through relationship and as a result of observations. The disciples . . . observed his actions, routines, reactions, and interactions . . . His disciples—both then and now—were

---

3. Bible quotations are from the NASB.
4. Boring, "Matthew," 260.
5. Bruce, *Colossians, Philemon, Ephesians*, 349–53.
6. Willard, "Spiritual Formation," 46.

to learn from his life as a living curriculum . . . Second, Jesus made disciples out of these followers through their constant exposure to his teachings. The most complete curriculum for disciples [is] the words, parables, sermons, prophecies, and teaching of Jesus.[7]

In other words, Jesus called his followers to observe his example and teaching that they might embody them themselves. As always, the ability to answer the conscientious disciple's question, "what would Jesus do?" naturally depends on a familiarity with what Jesus himself actually did.[8]

Of course, this sort of direct, face-to-face regimen with Jesus is no longer available this side of the Ascension. Things have changed; the Master has withdrawn. But Christians are not thereby utterly cut off from the informing example and teachings of Christ. Rather, in the words of the Gospels, the church is presented with a window that allows us to peer through the otherwise opaque walls of time to see our Lord and Savior as he was: alternatingly challenging and comforting, uniformly inspiring and compelling, and just a bit mysterious. The "living curriculum" that is Jesus' life perseveres, only now it is found not traveling the dusty roads of Palestine but contained in the Christian Scriptures.

## Evangelicalism's Problem

Still, even with the vital connection to Jesus available to us in the Gospels and all the formative benefits that holds out to us, spiritual formation is simply not something that modern Evangelical congregations generally pursue in a well-integrated, systematic fashion. To be sure, this is not to say that today's Evangelicals do not seek spiritual formation *at all*. Quite the contrary, vast amounts of time and effort are often expended within Evangelical circles to increase the theological awareness, moral rectitude, and Christian commitment of church members—all matters that might legitimately fall under the larger

---

7. Spencer, *Mere Churchianity*, 155.
8. Augsburger, *Dissident Discipleship*, 29. Also, Reuschling, *Reviving Evangelical Ethics*, 123.

umbrella of spiritual formation. Indeed, much of this work is done with the words and deeds of Jesus front and center. But, at least in the modern milieu, these efforts are often sporadic, disconnected from each other, and largely *ad hoc*: a small group study on prayer here, a sermon series on *The Purpose Driven Life* there, and so on. Thus spiritual formation, at least as a systematic and integrated concern, is mostly lacking in today's Evangelical churches.[9] Indeed, with the slow decline in the popularity of Sunday school, this issue has become increasingly acute.

This scarcity of integrated spiritual formation among Evangelicals has, in its own way, contributed to stereotypes of the movement as at times faddish, shallow, and cynically pragmatic.[10] After all, every church seeks to pursue a number of different and potentially competing interests. And without a sustained, conscientious focus on spiritual maturation, other concerns (such as the always pressing need for church growth) can come to shape the overall *stance* of a congregation. And this possibility, if allowed to develop unchecked, can lead churches in bizarre directions and dilute their distinctly Christian character.[11]

Even within reasonably healthy churches, however, a lack of sustained and systematic spiritual formation is a liability. By leaping from one program to the next, or one isolated sermon to the next, ministers can unintentionally overlook needed elements of Christian discipleship: What does a deeply Christian response to periods of loss and disappointment look like? How might a Christian manage hope that is orientated towards a long-distant fulfillment? Where ought one to look for humility in the midst of triumph? These kinds of questions simply may not be answered in the context of a five-week sermon series on tithing or family

9. Demarest, "New Dimensions," 375.
10. Recall James Twitchell's summary evaluation of mega-churches (themselves almost exclusively Evangelical and often Baptist) as "shallow, self-centered, corporatized, ahistorical, sensational, predictable, ceaselessly energetic, and a little paranoid" (Twitchell, *Shopping for God*, 284).
11. For some of the more prominent (and at times tragically comic) examples of this dynamic, see Spencer, *Mere Churchianity*, 29–32.

relationships—and yet they remain vitally important. Indeed, since spiritual formation is, as Henri Nouwen said, something oriented toward a person's heart (one's attitudes, affections, will, and so on) more than any external deed he or she might perform, all the well-intended and well-executed "how to" sermons and devotionals in the world may touch on such matters only tangentially.[12]

Clearly, something more is needed. Some sort of *sustained process* of Christocentric spiritual formation that seeks to engender comprehensive spiritual maturity is required in many Evangelical churches.

## A Way Forward

It is at the point of confluence of the above-mentioned realities—Evangelicalism's great need for sustained spiritual formation, the vital importance of a Christocentric focus, and the accessibility of Christ in the pages of Scripture—that the traditional Christian Calendar emerges as a possible solution.[13]

The Christian Calendar represents the end result of a long process of development, one that had its origins in the first-century Jewish calendar of biblical feast days (e.g., Passover, etc.) that were reinterpreted by Apostolic and Patristic Christians in a Christocentric fashion and then further expanded upon by later thinkers.[14] It is precisely towards Jesus' actions and his teachings as recorded in the New Testament that the Christian Calendar orients a believer. With its variegated seasons of devotion and its sacred holidays, the Christian Calendar moves the church through the major portions of Jesus' life, calling attention to what he did and what he said in an intentional variety of contexts and moods. Of course, the Christian Calendar is not a monolithic reality; different churches in different cultures have developed it in slightly different ways. Here in the West, though, the broad outlines at least are fairly consistent across

---

12. Nouwen, Christensen, and Laird, *Spiritual Formation*, xvii–xviii.
13. Harmon, *Towards Baptist Catholicity*, 159.
14. Stern, "Calendar."

denominational lines: In Advent, Christians place themselves alongside the ancient Israelites as they anticipated the arrival of the Messiah. In Christmas we celebrate his birth and the tenderness and gravity it entailed. In Epiphany we attend to the beginnings of Jesus' public ministry with all their promise and success, a focus that culminates in Transfiguration Sunday. In Lent, Christians follow Jesus as he finds himself opposed with ever greater vigor and tenacity, advancing towards the cross. In Holy Week—Palm Sunday, Maunday Thursday, Good Friday—we marvel as the Lord gives his very life for the sake of his divine mission. And in Easter we revel in Christ's victory over death and the dizzying possibilities that event holds for the human condition all the way through to a celebration of the Ascension.

In each of these seasons the faithful are encouraged to focus upon a different aspect of Jesus' life and character, and thus we come to have a fuller awareness of the man in all his complexity. Sermons, studies, devotionals, hymns—even the very decorations present in a church's sanctuary—can all be orientated around the season at hand, conspiring to drive home some particular facet of Jesus' person with reference to episodes from his life and the teachings he propounded.

The Christian Calendar isn't simply a tool of education, however, offering Christians mere data for curiosity's sake. Rather, by focusing on the fully-orbed life that Jesus lived through this intentional, repeated annual cycle, Christians come to inhabit the story of Jesus—living in it that it might live in us;[15] or, to use the familiar biblical expression, *abiding* in Christ that he might abide in us. As J. Winston Pearce opined in a remarkable passage,

> As the human life of Jesus unfolds through the Christian Year, from Advent through Easter and Pentecost, our lives are caught up in the procession. We are impressed with the similarity between his life and ours, yet we are shocked at the contrast between the way he lived his life and the way we live ours. His life unfurls before us: helpless infancy, disciplined and obedient youth, work and growth, choice and

---

15. Gross, *Living the Christian Year*, 16. Also, see German's conclusion in German, "Christian Year," 238.

temptation, vocation and ministry, Holy Week and resurrection. It is all there to see and, if we dare, experience! We begin to understand as season after season, year after year, we see Christ tempted, betrayed, crucified, buried, raised, and glorified before our eyes, as Paul would put it! We vicariously identify with him.[16]

With this dynamic in mind, the benefits offered by the Christian Calendar as pertain to spiritual formation are obvious. Instead of moving from one disconnected sermon series or Bible study to the next, a church moves though a year-long program oriented towards the organic and cumulative experiences of Jesus. Rather than focusing exclusively only on those themes most agreeable to the human heart, a church maturely faces all of Christ's life—even the sorrowful periods. And by seeing how the Lord responded to the ups and the downs of his experience, Christians come to possess a more comprehensive theological and existential grammar to sustain and encourage them when faced with similar circumstances. Indeed, through the observance of the Christian Calendar (whether in connection with the use of a lectionary or not), a church's entire experience of "doing church" can be rendered less self-involved and more theologically and christologically grounded. And through this shift in focus, a church can guard against the sort of ennui that may grow in an overly consumer-oriented Evangelical worship setting and that itself militates against spiritual maturity.[17]

## Evangelical Openness to the Calendar

Given Evangelicalism's traditionally low-church character and general distrust of ritual and formalism—elements only amplified in, for example, self-consciously Baptist congregations—one might expect Evangelical churches to balk at the idea of observing the historical Christian Calendar in any kind of detail. Christmas and Easter—sure; Lent and Epiphany—no, thank you.

---

16. Pearce, *Planning Your Preaching*, 42–43.
17. Rah, *The Next Evangelicalism*, 35–39. For a specific case study see Webber, *Evangelicals on the Canterbury Trail*, 109–10.

To be sure, such an expectation is not entirely without warrant. Still, Evangelicalism is gradually warming to the benefits of long-standing Christian traditions, traditions like the Christian Calendar.[18]

Since I am a Baptist pastor, let me speak in more detail here about Baptists. Consider that, historically speaking, even the few modest observances of the Christian Calendar common in today's Baptist churches (Christmas and Easter) represent a generally unnoticed softening and opening of Baptists to the calendar. Surprising as it may seem, there was a time—and that not too very long ago—when even these much beloved holidays were anathema in most Baptist circles. In his fascinating article on the topic, R. E. E. Harkness chronicles how representative and sometimes even authoritative voices in Baptist life across a broad geographical range in the eighteenth and nineteenth centuries referred to Christmas as "popemas," condemned the celebration of Easter as just so much "baptized paganism," and even insinuated that those who observe these holidays are "worshippers of the beast in these particulars."[19] That such comments are likely to strike modern Baptists as bizarre and even perhaps shocking indicates just how far we have come in these matters. Not only do we not share the scruples of our denominational forefathers here, most of us are totally unaware of their relevant views to begin with.

While the Baptist appropriation of Easter and Christmas was largely unconscious and the result of cultural assimilation, more recently work has been done that may facilitate additional progress in these matters—and that in a conscientious way this time. On an academic level, in partial continuity with past thinkers such as J. Winston Pearce of Golden Gate Baptist Theological Seminary and Robert E. Webber of Wheaton College, several Evangelical scholars of a Baptist stripe have emerged who seek to re-engage long-standing historical patterns of Christian worship and belief while still remaining within their own

---

18. Van Dyk, "The Church," 132–33.
19. Harkness, "Attitude of American Baptists," 325, 360.

denominational spheres.[20] These "Bapto-Catholics" (or "catholic Baptists" if one prefers) include such figures as Curtis Freeman of Duke University, Paul Fiddes of Oxford University, Ralph C. Wood, D. H. Williams, and Barry Harvey of Baylor University, Steven Harmon—recently of Beeson Divinity School but now teaching at Gardner-Webb University—and quite a few others. Each of these scholars has, in his own way, done the conceptual prep-work for legitimating the adoption of such practices as observing the fuller Christian Calendar within Evangelical contexts. And while it has been claimed (at times by these men themselves) that the agenda pursued by these and similar thinkers has not made much of an impact at the level of the local church,[21] the evidence points in a different direction, especially if one looks to the larger Evangelical universe.

In 2007, *U.S. News and World Report* noted an on-going traditionalist shift in worship among a number of religious communities, Evangelicalism included.[22] The *Washington Post* followed suit in 2008 by issuing its own observations on the re-appropriation of traditional liturgical practices at the local level by Evangelical Christians.[23] In that same year, even Evangelicalism's own flagship magazine, *Christianity Today*, published an issue, the cover story of which detailed precisely the phenomenon in view here: Evangelicals (particularly those of a younger generation) seeking a greater sense of spiritual depth and rootedness in the observances and disciplines of the ancient Christian church, and that within the context of local congregations.[24]

---

20. Jorgenson, "Bapto-Catholicism." Also, Cary, "Authority, Unity and Truthfulness," 22–39.
21. "Thus far interest in a catholic Baptist programme of retrieval has been almost exclusively limited to academic theologians. The current state of affairs might lead some to regard this discussion as . . . of little consequence for the warp and woof of Baptist church life" (Harmon, *Towards Baptist Catholicity*, 19–20).
22. Tolson, "Return to Tradition."
23. Salmon, "Feeling Renewed."
24. Armstrong, "Future Lies in the Past."

The somewhat pessimistic status reports of Bapto-Catholic seminary professors notwithstanding then, it seems that an Evangelical interest in historical Christian thought and worship does indeed extend beyond the walls of the academy. The time is ripe, then, for a further appropriation of the Christian Calendar among Baptists, one that goes beyond merely Christmas and Easter to embrace the totality of Christ's life as he lived it and as we can relive it together in the midst of Christian worship.

*Personal Experience*

I recently completed a six-year pastoral tenure at the First Baptist Church of Granada Hills in Los Angeles, CA. During my time there I felt moved by the above considerations to integrate the Christian Calendar into the church's worship. Working in conjunction with the Women's Missionary Union I designed seasonal banners and paraments in keeping with the traditional liturgical colors and themes. I began utilizing a lectionary (i.e., the Revised Common Lectionary) to ensure that my preaching would be appropriate for the season at hand. And, each Sunday from mid-November until about a month after Easter, the First Baptist Church focused on Jesus Christ intentionally, methodically, and episodically in the context of our worship for the glory of God and the building up of the faithful.

While there were questions from time to time, and the occasional expression of skepticism, this new (and yet quite old) element of our spiritual formation was, generally speaking, well received. Members of the church appreciated the greater sense of significance attached to time. They came to recognize the importance of honoring and modeling *all* of Christ's life by facing *all* of his life in turn.

Perhaps no other element related to the Christian Calendar was so heartily embraced there as the observance of Good Friday. Whereas in the past, Easter Sunday (of course) featured a sermon on the resurrection of Jesus, the story of the crucifixion was either awkwardly appended to the Palm Sunday sermon or only briefly mentioned as a preamble on Easter itself. The inadequacy of this arrangement was apparent to all and as such the congregation was quite enthusiastic about setting some time aside to focus exclusively on Jesus' great sacrifice in the midst of a distinct (and distinctly somber) service. Indeed, the attendance at that night-time service rivaled that at even some of our Sunday morning programs.

My own experience at the First Baptist Church of Granada Hills stands thus as evidence that, in the world of Evangelicalism, the Christian Calendar and its related traditions are not merely the playthings of ivory tower academics but that they are also workable solutions in local churches as well.

*Conclusion*

Of course, the Christian Calendar is not a magic bullet. It does not, in and of itself, guarantee rigorous and reliable spiritual formation within those congregations that observe it. Nevertheless, as one tool among many—and as a profoundly christocentric tool at that—the Christian Calendar is a helpful option for those Evangelical churches willing to employ it. Given that the need for spiritual formation is ever-present, given further that Evangelicals in particular stand in need of additional tools here, and given that a growing number of Evangelicals are seemingly open to such a tool as this, it may be hoped that the Christian Calendar shall become a commonplace in Evangelical churches —including Baptist churches—in the coming years.

*Bibliography*

Armstrong, Chris. "The Future Lies in the Past: Why Evangelicals Are Connecting with the Early Church as They Move into the 21st Century." *Christianity Today*, February 2008, 22–29.

Augsburger, David. *Dissident Discipleship: A Spirituality of Self-Surrender, Love of God, and Love of Neighbor*. Grand Rapids: Brazos, 2006.

Borchert, Gerald L. "John." In *Mercer Commentary on the Bible*, edited by Watson E. Mills and Richard F. Wilson, 1043–82. Macon, GA: Mercer University Press, 1995.

Boring, M. Eugene. "Matthew." In *The New Interpreter's Bible: A Commentary in Twelve Volumes*, edited by Leander E. Keck et al., 8:87–505. Nashville: Abingdon, 1995.

Bruce, F. F. *The Epistles to the Colossians, to Philemon, and to the Ephesians*. The New International Commentary on the New Testament. Edited by Gordon D. Fee. Grand Rapids: Eerdmans, 1984.

Cary, Jeffrey W. "Authority, Unity and Truthfulness: The Body of Christ in the Theologies of Robert Jenson and Rowan Williams with a View toward Implications for Free Church Ecclesiology." PhD diss., Baylor University, 2010.

Demarest, Bruce A. "New Dimensions in Spirituality and Christianity Living." In *New Dimensions in Evangelical Thought: Essays in Honor of Millard J. Erickson*, edited by David S. Dockery, 374–93. Downers Grove, IL: InterVarsity, 1998.

German, T. J. "Christian Year." In *The Evangelical Dictionary of Theology*. 2nd ed., edited by Walter A. Elwell, 236–38. Grand Rapids: Baker Academic, 2001.

Gross, Bobby. *Living the Christian Year: Time to Inhabit the Story of God*. Downers Grove, IL: InterVarsity, 2009.

Harkness, R. E. E. "Attitude of American Baptists to Church Holy Days." *The Crozer Quarterly* 7 (1930) 351–66.

Harmon, Steven R. *Towards Baptist Catholicity: Essays on Tradition and the Baptist Vision*. Studies in Baptist History and Thought 27. Eugene, OR: Wipf & Stock, 2006.

Jorgenson, Cameron H. "Bapto-Catholicism: Recovering Tradition and Reconsidering the Baptist Identity." PhD diss., Baylor University, 2008.

Köstenberger, Andreas J. *Encountering John*. Grand Rapids: Baker Academic, 1999.

Nouwen, Henri, Michael J. Christensen, and Rebecca J. Laird. *Spiritual Formation: Following the Movements of the Spirit*. New York: HarperOne, 2010.

Pearce, J. Winston. *Planning Your Preaching*. Nashville: Broadman, 1979.

Rah, Soong-chan. *The Next Evangelicalism: Freeing the Church from Western Cultural Captivity*. Downers Grove, IL: InterVarsity, 2009.

Reuschling, Wyndy Corbin. *Reviving Evangelical Ethics: The Promises and Pitfalls of Classic Models of Morality*. Grand Rapids: Brazos, 2008.

Salmon, Jacqueline L. "Feeling Renewed by Ancient Traditions." *Washington Post*, March 8, 2008, B09. Online http://www.washingtonpost.com/wp-dyn/content/article/2008/03/07/AR2008030702925.html?sid=ST2008030731 13.

Spencer, Michael. *Mere Churchianity: Finding Your Way Back to Jesus-Shaped Spirituality*. Colorado Springs, CO: Waterbrook, 2010.

Stern, Sacha. "Calendar." In *A Dictionary of Jewish-Christian Relations*, edited by Edward Kessler and Neil Wenborn, 71–72. New York: Cambridge University Press, 2005.

Tolson, Jay. "A Return to Tradition: A New Interest in Old Ways Takes Root in Catholicism and Many Other Faiths." *U.S. News and World Report*, December 13, 2007, 42–48.

Online: http://www.usnews.com/news/national/articles/2007/12/13/a-return-to-tradition.

Twitchell, James B. *Shopping for God: How Christianity Went from in Your Heart to in Your Face*. New York: Simon & Schuster, 2007.

Van Dyk, Leanne. "The Church in Evangelical Theology and Practice." In *The Cambridge Companion to Evangelical Theology*, edited by Timothy Larsen and Daniel J. Treier, 125–44. New York: Cambridge University Press, 2007.

Webber, Robert E. *Evangelicals on the Canterbury Trail: Why Evangelicals Are Attracted to the Liturgical Church*. Harrisburg, PA: Morehouse, 1989.

Willard, Dallas. "Spiritual Formation in Christ Is for the Whole Life and the Whole Person." In *For All the Saints: Evangelical Theology and Christian Spirituality*, edited by Timothy George and Alister McGrath, 39–53. Louisville: Westminster John Knox, 2003.

CANADIAN THEOLOGICAL EDUCATION IN THE TWENTY-FIRST
CENTURY—AN UPDATE AND EVALUATION[1]

Stanley E. Porter
McMaster Divinity College, Hamilton, ON, Canada

*Introduction and Method*

In a supplementary volume of the *Toronto Journal of Theology* on The Future of Theological Education in Canada, published in 2009, I analyzed and examined the crisis in which theological education in Canada was then mired.[2] In that paper, I examined all of the types of institutions represented by CHEC (Christian Higher Education Canada), including Bible colleges, Christian universities, seminaries, and graduate schools—although I concentrated upon seminaries and graduate schools. Tracing the variety of statistics available up to the 2006–2007 academic year,

---

1. This paper was presented and discussed at the first "Canadian Seminaries: Challenges and Opportunities," Pre-Forum Conference, Christian Higher Education Canada National Forum: For Christ and His Kingdom: Inspiring a New Generation, King's University College, Edmonton, 28 May 2012. Christian Higher Education Canada (CHEC) is an association of thirty-two Christ-centered institutions of higher education in Canada. I have been an active supporter of CHEC, serving on the amalgamation team and as a council member, board member, secretary of the board, and its chair. I was secretary of the board when I delivered this paper, but the views are my own.

2. This initial paper was first delivered at a conference of the Churches' Council on Theological Education in Canada, entitled "Who Do We Think We Are? Re-Mapping Theological Education in Canada in the 21st Century," on 8 November 2007. At that conference I was invited to speak because of my connections to CHEC, although the opinions were, of course, my own (as they are here). This paper was published as Porter, "Theological Education." There are other papers in this supplement to the *Toronto Journal of Theology* that address Canadian theological education, but none deals with the statistical trends.

I chronicled a decline in enrollment among Christian seminaries and graduate schools in Canada, in conjunction with increased strain on financial resources as a result, as most institutions are tuition driven. I then challenged seminaries and graduate schools to consider means of addressing these problems. Finally, I addressed the issue of culture, analyzing the results of the 2007 Ipsos-Reid poll sponsored by CHEC and the Evangelical Fellowship of Canada. I basically found that Canadian theological education is a relatively small entity within its much larger context of Canadian society, with a number of inherent limitations that it must face.

When I wrote that first paper—to date the only paper I know of that has examined the contemporary Christian educational scene in Canada in such statistical detail—I did not know that the economic crisis of 2008 was upon us. Nor did I know that the Association of Theological Schools (ATS), the accrediting body for most seminaries throughout North America, would begin to focus so much upon competency-based assessment, in direct response to the pressures of its own accrediting agency, the Council for Higher Education Accreditation, and the United States Department of Education. Nevertheless, these two things did happen.

This paper revisits the situation in Canadian theological education, focusing almost exclusively upon seminaries. Many of the challenges that I identified in my original paper have become worse, especially in relation to two major areas: finances, due to inadequate financial models; and decreasing student numbers, which translates into tuition revenue (so again, finances). Other areas of concern include a slowness to implement curriculum review and revision, on the part of both ATS and individual institutions, and failure to attract wider attention within our contexts. Despite these difficulties, one of the areas not successfully pursued has been significant partnerships and mergers. It appears that many of our institutions have considered it better to slowly hang separately than to hang together (to paraphrase a quotation attributed to Benjamin Franklin).

In this paper, I examine the two major areas that I discussed before—critical numbers and curriculum—and see where Canadian seminary education now stands in relation to where it was only six short years before. Then, I add two new sections, one on implications in terms of indestructible institutions and another on avenues for further consideration.

## Critical Numbers in Canadian Seminaries

My earlier paper had limited accessible data. I now have a more accessible source, using ATS's 2011–2012 Annual Data Tables as the data base for my analyses. I deal with two sets of critical numbers—student numbers and financial numbers.

Canada now has 39 of the 260 ATS fully accredited, candidate, and associate seminaries (Table 1.1-A of the ATS 2011–2012 Annual Data Tables, hereafter cited in this format). When I surveyed the situation earlier, Canada had 35 of 252 such institutions.[3] This means that half of the additional institutions within ATS are Canadian (4 of 8)! This also means that Canada continues to have more seminaries per capita than the United States. The Stats Can website indicates that Canada now has 34,795,416 people (previously 33,165,087). This means there is an average of one seminary per 892,190 people, a decrease of around 5,000 people per seminary than four years ago (at 947,574). The United States, by contrast, with its 221 seminaries, functions within a population of 312,780,968 (previously 301,139,947), or roughly one seminary per 1,415,298, an increase in the number of people per seminary from last time (1,387,742). Seminaries in the United States have more people potentially supporting them than previously. Seminaries in the United States also now have over 50% more people per seminary available to draw upon than do those in Canada. From the outset, we see that Canadian theological education is moving in the wrong direction—Canada is adding

---

3. I realize that there are some anomalies in ATS statistics, but cannot hope to address these on the basis of my limited information. One clear oddity is that there are two institutions listed among the Canadian institutions that have no reported students, the Toronto School of Theology and University of Winnipeg School of Theology (apparently because they are reported elsewhere). The United States has several such institutions as well.

seminaries at a rate that decreases the number of potential people per seminary for support, just the opposite of the United States. This has direct implications in two major areas—the number of students potentially available for seminary education, and the number of potential donors to such institutions. Those in Canada have a decreasing base of people for both, whereas the United States is growing in support.

I now turn to the number of seminary students within Canada and the United States. According to my initial report, in 2006 a total of 82,279 students were enrolled in ATS institutions. That number has decreased each year since, so that in 2011 (for the 2011–2012 academic year) a total of 74,193 are enrolled (Tables 2.2-A, B, C). This represents a decline of roughly 10% over six years. Whereas in 2006 there were 6,385 enrolled in Canadian institutions, in 2011 that number had decreased to 5,234. That is a decrease of about 19% or nearly 200 students per year on average. In my original article, on the basis of observation of only a limited number of years, I estimated that "if the downward movement continues at the same rate, in a mere five years there will be fewer than 5000 students in seminary in Canada."[4] I missed it slightly. If the downward trend continues, next year Canadian seminary students will have decreased to below 5000 students. This means that Canadians attend seminary as a percentage of national population at a rate of .015% (down from .019%), in contrast to the United States, where people attend seminary at a rate of .022% (also down from .025%). Within Canada, the average size of an ATS seminary is now 134 total students per institution (141 if the two institutions with no reported enrollment are excluded; down from 182 students six years ago), compared to 312 in the United States (itself down from roughly 350 students six years ago). The United States itself is experiencing a downward trend in seminary enrollment, but it is not nearly as great a decrease as in Canada.

So far, we have been dealing with rough overall figures. The distribution of these figures across institutions is worth examining in more detail.

---

4. Porter, "Theological Education," 46.

### TABLE 1
### Distribution of ATS Institutions by Total Head Count for All Schools
### From ATS 2011–2012 Annual Data Table 1.4-A

| Head Count | Number of Institutions | % of All Schools |
| --- | --- | --- |
| Under 75 | 39 | 15% |
| 75–150 | 84 | 32.3% |
| 151–300 | 73 | 28.1% |
| 301–500 | 32 | 12.3% |
| 501–1000 | 17 | 6.5% |
| Over 1000 | 12 | 4.5% |
| No Report | 3 | 1.2% |

Comparison with 2006 indicates that there are ten more institutions in the under 75 category (29 before), sixteen more in the 75-150 category (68 before), and fewer institutions in each of the other categories (seven fewer in 151-300 from 80; nine fewer in 301-500 from 41; two fewer in 501-1000 from 19; and one fewer in over 1000 from 13). This indicates that there is an increase in smaller institutions and decrease in larger institutions, over the last six years.

By comparison, Canadian institutions do not follow exactly the same overall pattern, but there is room for concern nevertheless.

### TABLE 2
### Distribution of ATS Institutions by Total Head Count for Canadian Schools
### Based on ATS 2011–2012 Annual Data Table 1.4-C

| Head Count | Number of Institutions | % of Canadian Schools |
| --- | --- | --- |
| Under 75 | 13 | 33.3% |
| 75–150 | 9 | 23.1% |
| 151–300 | 13 | 33.3% |
| 301–500 | 1 | 2.6% |
| 501–1000 | 1 | 2.6% |
| No Report | 2 | 5.1% |

A comparison with 2006 reveals that there are four more institutions in the under 75 category (9 before), one less in the 75-150 category (10 before), two more in the 151-300 category (11 before), but two less in the 301-500 category (3 before) and one less in the 501-1000 category (2 before). There has been a clear retraction in overall numbers, including in the larger institutions, with only two Canadian institutions now exceeding 300 total headcount, whereas there were five before.

These figures can be further refined, to give a more precise estimation of where CHEC institutions stand in relation to the other Canadian theological institutions. I use the standard ATS differentiation of institutions on the basis of being evangelical, mainline Protestant, or Roman Catholic (although this is not indicated in the statistics themselves). Of the 39 ATS seminaries within Canada, evangelical seminaries number thirteen, of which eleven are CHEC members (if my calculations are correct), seventeen are mainline Protestant, and seven are Roman Catholic, whereas two are interdenominational (these two have no students, so they do not affect the statistics).[5] Evangelical students within ATS institutions account for 2,755 of the total number of students in graduate theological education within Canada, or 53% of the total number of students (a decrease from 56%), with an average size of 212 total students enrolled in each seminary (well down from the 254 total students of six years ago). Mainline Protestant seminaries have a total of 1,614 students, or 31% of the total, with an average size of 95 total students enrolled (down from 112 six years ago). Roman Catholic institutions have a total of 865 students, or 16% of the total, with an average institutional size of 124 total students (significantly down from the 207 students of six years ago). These are not encouraging figures. In my previous paper, I wondered out loud whether it was possible for a seminary with a total headcount of 112 to continue to be viable (mainline Protestant), but 95 students (the

---

5. See ATS 2011–2012 Annual Data Table 1.2, "Significant Institutional Characteristics of Each Member School, 2011–2012" in the Annual Data Tables, for much of the information regarding enrollment, full-time equivalent, and long-term investment.

current figure) seems perilously inadequate, with the Roman Catholic institutions now becoming similarly precarious. Evangelical institutions are doing better, but only marginally, as the average total has fallen significantly, to the point, I believe, of raising serious concern.

In my previous paper, I was unable to calculate the full-time equivalent statistics. I am now able to do so, although without the comparative figures used above. What I have been outlining above is total headcount. There is a significant difference between total headcount and full-time equivalent, and it is the full-time equivalent that has a direct relationship to tuition revenue. The 5,234 total headcount of ATS seminary students translates into only 2,746 full-time equivalent students.[6] In other words, if each student were taking a minimal full load (and assuming, for the sake of discussion, that this is calculated similarly), there are only 2,746 full-time students taking advanced theological studies in ATS institutions in all of Canada.

The distribution of full-time equivalent students across types of theological institution is also interesting. The evangelical institutions account for 1,396 of these full-time equivalents, or 51%, with an average size of 107 full-time equivalent students per institution. In other words, evangelical institutions may have a larger headcount, but these convert to fewer full-time equivalents than they do in other institutions. The mainline Protestant institutions have 895 full-time equivalents, or 32%, a slight increase in percentage over their head count, with an average size of 53 full-time equivalent students. Roman Catholic institutions account for 455 full-time equivalents, or 16%, with an average size of 65 full-time equivalent students per institution. These figures indicate a number of very small institutions.

A further examination of the distribution of institutions according to full-time equivalent over all ATS institutions provides further insight.

---

6. There seems to be a slight discrepancy between the figures presented in Table 2.3-C of the ATS 2011–2012 Annual Data Tables, which presents the total full-time equivalent enrollment as 2,738, and my own calculations.

TABLE 3
Distribution of ATS Institutions by Full-Time Equivalent for All Schools
From ATS 2011–2012 Annual Data Table 1.5-A

| Full-Time Equivalent | Number of Institutions | % of All Schools |
| --- | --- | --- |
| Under 75 | 80 | 30.8% |
| 75–150 | 91 | 35.0% |
| 151–300 | 46 | 17.7% |
| 301–500 | 22 | 8.5% |
| 501–1000 | 11 | 4.2% |
| Over 1000 | 7 | 2.7% |
| No Report | 3 | 1.2% |

As discussed above, when considering total enrollment, there is an increase since 2006 in the number of institutions under 75 by eleven (from 69) and from 75-150 by fourteen (from 77). As would be expected, there is a fall in number of institutions from 151-300 by fifteen (from 61), from 301-500 by one (from 23), and from 501-1000 by two (from 13). There is an increase by two in institutions over 1000 (from 5).

A comparison of only Canadian institutions on the basis of full-time equivalent students is even more troubling.

TABLE 4
Distribution of ATS Institutions by Full-Time Equivalent
for Canadian Schools
From ATS 2011–2012 Annual Data Table 1.5-C

| Full-Time Equivalent | Number of Institutions | % of Canadian Schools |
| --- | --- | --- |
| Under 75 | 22 | 54.6% |
| 75–150 | 12 | 30.8% |
| 151–300 | 2 | 5.1% |
| 301–500 | 1 | 2.6% |
| No Report | 2 | 5.1% |

As indicated above, when considering total enrollment, there is an increase in the number of institutions under 75 by four (from 18) and from 75-150 by one (from 11). There is a decrease in the other categories: from 151-300 by one (from 3), from 301-500 by one (from 2). This indicates that nearly 60% of the Canadian institutions are smaller than 75 full-time equivalent, and 87% (nearly 90%) are smaller than 150 full-time equivalent students.

These figures are disturbing in a number of ways. Most importantly, virtually all of the Canadian theological institutions are small. Evangelical institutions are the largest, but 107 full-time equivalent average is still a relatively small number of students, especially as it reflects a declining trend. Mainline Protestant and Roman Catholic institutions are in far worse shape (something I will say more about below). Some of the institutions that are included in these figures are distressingly small, and I must wonder whether they have the critical mass necessary to educate their students sufficiently well to merit accreditation as graduate level institutions. Among all the Canadian ATS institutions, there are ten institutions with 26 or fewer full-time equivalent, the lowest two with a mere six full-time equivalent each—only one evangelical institution is within this group of ten. This group of ten institutions, nevertheless, represents more than one-quarter of all of the ATS accredited seminaries in Canada. Second, as we all know, the cost of processing a part-time student is just about the same as that of a full-time student. However, with such low numbers of full-time equivalent students overall, the total tuition resources are very limited, even though institutions are processing a far larger number of students, and it further raises the question of sustainability.

There is, I believe, increasing realization over the last five or so years that there is no viable or sustainable financial model for higher education, to say nothing of theological education. Whereas the typical business model involves sales of product versus expenses to provide said product, education follows a different model. Every educational model developed so far seems to require some form of outside income source besides the money generated through tuition, even those with endowments (the source of the endowment being an outside income source, such as gifts or bequests). This is certainly true of Canadian provincial universities, whose financial models are dependent upon the provincial government providing a large portion of their operating funding. The same is true of private institutions, such as seminaries, with the exception that they usually do not have the opportunity to benefit from taxpayer dollars in the same way that provincial universities do. There are a few seminaries that do benefit from either direct or indirect governmental support, often channeled through a larger institution, such as a university (my institution receives a small portion of money in this way, even though it is fully independent). For most theological institutions, especially evangelical institutions, however, their primary source of income is tuition revenue. I do not have specific figures (and do not know if such figures are available), but the range of tuition revenue for Canadian theological institutions as a part of general operations probably extends from 30% upwards, with many of our institutions being considered tuition-driven institutions, that is, those that are primarily dependent upon tuition revenue for their financial existence. This is entirely appropriate, in that it gives these institutions an indication of whether as institutions they are providing the kind of training sought by students, and hence by the church, if they can recruit students to their programs and if students go out from their institutions and fulfill their appointed roles. However, tuition revenue, as we all realize, is itself unstable. Long-term planning is made more difficult because fluctuations in tuition (and the underlying student numbers) mean that an institution will have to adjust to an unusually large or small year of incoming students, which will need to work its way through the institution during the longevity of the program. More importantly, if the trends that I noted above continue, then the tuition revenue stream will continue to shrink for most institutions, while our costs will continue to grow, so that income and expenses will begin to diverge at an alarming rate. If the indicators above are not remedied, reliance upon tuition revenue as a source of long-term financial growth or even sustainability will become increasingly difficult. Tuition is clearly the major source of revenue for most evangelical institutions.

Another source of income is endowment-generated income. ATS provides some useful information regarding endowments. Reporting of long-term investments allows examination of the endowments of ATS institutions—although this does not indicate how much income is generated by these endowments (see Table 1.2 in the 2011–2012 Annual Data Tables). The results are as follows:

TABLE 5
Investment Holdings of All Canadian ATS Schools
(amount in millions of dollars)
From ATS 2011–2012 Annual Data Table 1.2

| Amount | Number of Institutions | % of Canadian Inst. |
|---|---|---|
| Above 19.9 | 2 | 5% |
| 15-19.9 | 2 | 5% |
| 10-14.9 | 4 | 10% |
| 5-9.9 | 7 | 18% |
| Up to 4.9 | 11 | 28% |
| 0 | 13 | 33% |

One-third of all of the ATS accredited seminaries in Canada have no significant endowments. Nearly two-thirds of the institutions (61%) have under 5 million dollars in endowments. Only two have endowments over 19.9 million, one at 20 million and the other at 21 million.

TABLE 6
Investment Holdings of Canadian Evangelical ATS Schools
(amount in millions of dollars)
From ATS 2011–2012 Annual Data Table 1.2

| Amount | Number of Institutions | % of Canadian Inst. |
|---|---|---|
| Above 19.9 | 1 | 8% |
| 15-19.9 | 1 | 8% |
| 10-14.9 | 1 | 8% |
| 5-9.9 | 2 | 15% |
| Up to 4.9 | 2 | 15% |
| 0 | 6 | 46% |

The situation is similarly bad for evangelical institutions, where nearly half of them have no endowment funds, and again nearly two-thirds (61%) have under 5 million dollars.

These figures reveal several important, yet perhaps not readily self-evident, facts. The major one is that many if not most of these institutions, whether Canadian-wide or specifically evangelical, are almost assuredly dependent upon sources of income that do not include endowment income (or tuition). Three major sources need to be mentioned—one is annual fund giving or contributions, another is denominational support, and a third is larger institutional (and perhaps directly or indirectly governmental) support.

A number of institutions rely upon direct or indirect governmental support. Institutions that enjoy this support are particularly vulnerable, I believe, because such support will almost assuredly come to an end—perhaps sooner rather than later—because of larger financial constraints and increasing secularization in Canadian society. The situation only requires that it become known to the wider taxpaying populace—or their elected representatives—that Christian theological seminaries, and especially evangelical ones, are receiving taxpayer money to educate Christian clergy for this to be curtailed. In some ways, this is probably appropriate. One might make a case that an educated Christian clergy is a benefit to the overall society, but this argument is probably not sufficient. Other religions could make the same claim, and I think that most Christians would probably not want their tax dollars to fund educating such clergy. Further, I think that it is reasonable for Christians themselves, and their churches, to provide support for the training of their clergy, as it is not a governmental mandate. Other institutions, although probably few if any evangelical ones, receive direct affiliated institutional support. This would include institutions that are closely tied to a provincial university, where their assets are held by the larger institution. This too is a precarious situation for an institution to find itself in, as it is dependent upon the larger institution believing, and continuing to believe, that a theological institution is necessary for the larger life of the university.

As for denominational support, many of the 39 Canadian ATS institutions have strong denominational ties; however, several of these institutions are quite small in size. For example, two Lutheran Church of Canada institutions have only a relatively small number of students, the Southern Baptist theological seminary is about the same small size, and at least one Roman Catholic institution is quite small. I have only anecdotal evidence regarding denominational support of institutions, but if most denominational support is like that of mine, theological institutions will need to think seriously about their futures. My denomination only provides 2.8% of operating revenue. This amount has fallen progressively and dramatically since before my arrival at McMaster Divinity College in 2001. I suspect that some of the denominations will need to economize their support of their institutions. Over the last several years, the United Church of Canada, because of its plummeting church membership and hence decrease in need for clergy, has had to re-assess the future of its theological institutions (a task not yet complete), and the Anglicans may well need to do likewise. The Presbyterians may also find that two institutions is a luxury they cannot afford. Even the Roman Catholic institutions—some of them well supported by various structures, including generous bishops—may need to be reassessed, although their number in Canada has increased by two over the last five years (from 5 to 7).

Finally, general giving is the avenue that most institutions rely upon to make up the difference between their major source of income, usually tuition, and their solvency. In distinct ways, this is appropriate, as it reflects the ability of the institution to get its message out to its constituency and it gives this constituency an opportunity to respond in support of the institution. However, there are also some major problems with reliance upon this kind of support. One is the fact that such support is subject to the vagaries of the general financial climate. The last financial downturn in 2008 showed a general decrease in giving to educational institutions, including theological institutions, on both large and small scales. Such support may return in better financial times, but most institutions need such support on a year-by-year basis, and so waiting for more prosperous economic times, when economic cycles can take years to recover, puts them in a vulnerable financial position.

As a result, most institutions dream of having a large endowment as the cure of all financial problems. Harvard University is the envy of educational institutions worldwide, because of its nearly 30 billion dollar endowment. One has only to mention this phenomenal amount dedicated to supporting Harvard's educational endeavors to get sighs of envy from others in higher education. One can just hear administrators ask themselves, "What would it be like to have that kind of endowment?" I am in many ways fortunate to be the President of the institution that has the highest endowment of all of the 39 Canadian ATS institutions, with an endowment and other long-term investments of roughly 21 million dollars. This is not the 30 billion dollars of Harvard University, to be sure, but Harvard and McMaster Divinity College have some statistical similarities: our ratios of operational budget to size of endowment and to income produced by endowment are roughly the same. Harvard has an endowment of just short of 30 billion dollars in relation to an operating budget of about 4 billion dollars, producing about 40% of its income.[7] McMaster Divinity College has an endowment of 21 million dollars in relation to an operating budget of about 3 million dollars, producing an equivalent percentage. As a result, Harvard's endowment produces about the same proportion of annual operations for the University as our endowment does for our operations. Such an endowment is not, however, stress-free. Endowments also are subject to the fluctuations of the market, and if an institution is too reliant upon them, planning can be upset by both long- and short-term market variations. During the recent economic downturn, Harvard had to cancel some of its building projects, freeze salaries, and let many people go, because of the fall in its endowment value and hence the money available to spend. McMaster Divinity College, thankfully, did not do any of these things. Endowments are a good means of maintaining institutional stability, in that they provide a long-

---

7. For these facts, see Christensen and Eyring, *Innovative University*, pp. xxvii, 8; cf. 185–91.

term source of continued financial resources. However, they are not as flexible as sometimes needed during tough economic times, and are subject to market fluctuations. They also take a long time to build, and the drawdown is small (currently around 5%) in comparison to the total amount.

Whereas five years ago the situation for theological education both in the United States and in Canada was serious, it is now even more precarious. I do not want to catastrophize the predicament by saying that I think that theological education is on the brink of extinction. That would be too extreme. However, that does not mean that it will continue as it has in the past, or that it will not take much hard work on the part of all who are involved in it. In my previous article, I noted that it was Einstein who said that it is unreasonable to continue to do the same thing and expect a different result—some say this is the definition of insanity. I believe that it is clear that we must do some things differently. I will address some of those below in subsequent sections. Nevertheless, let me say here that whatever steps we have been taking do not show signs of effecting the kinds of changes that we need to reverse what is clearly a downward trend. In many institutions, we are perilously close to reaching a minimal threshold of sustainability in student numbers and probably also in other financial indicators. Increasing costs of living, staffing costs, infrastructure costs, and salaries, along with a realistic cap on the ability to increase tuition and find other forms of income, make it imperative that student numbers not decrease further. In fact, we need a significantly larger number of students involved in theological education to establish the kinds of critical numbers needed if we are to sustain all of the present institutions. However, we perhaps need to evaluate whether we require all of the current institutions. We have already seen the effects of decreasing student numbers. These include institutions whose financial sustainability has been jeopardized, to the point where they have been if not unable to continue, at least not able to continue as before. At the least, they will be unable to provide the kinds of faculty and support that students at the graduate level warrant and that are necessary for the kind of training that institutions are expected to provide. As I noted above, one of the avenues that has not been explored as a way of dealing with the issues raised here is strategic partnerships and mergers. Institutions across the spectrum of theological education in Canada have closed down, have forfeited accreditation, or have cut back radically on programs or in other areas, but to my knowledge no seminaries have engaged in successful merger or partnership to the point of creating a new, more viable institution. I will return to this issue below.

## Curriculum and the Canadian Seminary

Whereas the critical numbers reveal a situation that is distressing in the least, curriculum including both degrees offered and the construction of such degrees provides one means of addressing these difficulties. If our situation is serious, then why is it that so little is being done? There are several considerations to weigh.

The first is that theological education has for too long focused upon a single degree, the MDiv. The MDiv degree is a general-purpose theological degree that was designed as a post-baccalaureate degree for those who had a broad liberal arts education. There are a number of problems with this degree. One is that there are fewer and fewer theological students who come directly from a broad liberal arts degree and without any other kind of theological training or experience. More and more students in theological education are already working in ministry, and so have already gained valuable experience in both the knowledge and skills required for ministry. Many of these students, when they come to seminary, find that seminary is unnecessarily redundant, because of their accumulated experience, with few avenues for addressing this situation. There are some advanced placements that they can take advantage of, but very few other opportunities.

A second consideration is that their ministry experience means that they are often unable to undertake the degree as it was designed. The MDiv degree was originally designed as a three-year residential degree, more often than not undertaken by single men directly out of their undergraduate programs. Most people who attend seminary today are already experienced in ministry, and many of them are actively involved in some type of ministry. This both affects their ability to relocate for the purpose of education, and constricts their availability for undertaking the traditional theological curriculum. Efforts are being made to have modular courses, various types of reconfigured courses, and of course mediated learning through online offerings, but these are for the most part still designed to function in relation to the standard theological curriculum. The standard theological curriculum is at least as old as ATS itself. My academic dean tells me that Dan Aleshire, the executive director of ATS, has stated in public that the basic MDiv curriculum has not changed appreciably since ATS was instituted in the 1930s. My own investigation of the issue indicates that the standard theological curriculum may well be even older than that, going back to the Harvard Divinity School curriculum as developed during the late nineteenth and early twentieth centuries. It does not matter when the current curriculum was first developed, since the point is that it is an understatement to say that the curriculum of the MDiv, whether it is called by this name or by its predecessor, the BD, is static and inflexible. It emphasizes a series of introductory survey type courses in a world that increasingly demands subject-specific expertise. It is also patronizing and limiting for mature students who rightly expect to be able to make their own educational choices. I can think of no other subject area that has been as intransigent in development of curricular options as has the standard theological curriculum. All of the major professions, as well as most other academic areas, have shown far more willingness to creatively reconstruct and develop their curriculum than has the MDiv, the standard theological degree. This probably has a relationship to the decreasing number of people interested in pursuing this degree option.

There are some interesting and in some ways encouraging signs that some institutions are finding ways to circumvent the unnecessary constriction of the MDiv degree. One of these is to emphasize other degrees. ATS as an accrediting institution still continues (unnecessarily) to emphasize the MDiv, as is witnessed by their data-gathering itself, which places emphasis on the MDiv, and their numerous seminars and discussions that inevitably focus on the MDiv. However, ATS institutions, rightly, are attempting to break out of these confines. There are two trends that are most readily noticeable from the ATS data.

The first is the emphasis on advanced ministerial degrees. It should not come as a surprise that a number of Canadian institutions have followed what appears to be a long-standing trend in ATS institutions continent-wide in offering advanced ministerial degrees, presumably mostly the DMin. Of the 39 Canadian ATS institutions, I note that four of them emphasize advanced ministerial degrees to the point of these becoming the predominant degree offered by their institution (ATS 2011–2012 Annual Data Table 2.15). These include Acadia Divinity College, where there are 42 total students and 26 full-time equivalent in the MDiv, but 72 total students and 24 full-time equivalent in advanced ministerial degrees; Knox Theological College with 35/18 in the MDiv and 67/22 in advanced ministerial degrees; Providence Theological Seminary, with 17/9 in the MDiv and 26/9 in advanced ministerial degrees; and St. Stephen's College, with 0 students in the MDiv and 28/9 in advanced ministerial degrees. There was a time in the 1980s or so when it was thought that seminaries would follow the way of medical schools and law schools and make the first ministerial degree the DMin or equivalent. That movement did not catch on, so that the first degree is still the MDiv. Nevertheless, a number of institutions are offering advanced ministerial degrees and doing so quite successfully, including one that has no MDiv degree students. The history of the DMin, at least in Canada, is that it has had its ups and downs. There was a time when offering the DMin was a boom industry, but then the situation became quiescent, when one senior administrator was heard to say that "everyone who wants a DMin has one." There are now apparently others who want them, so some institutions are pursuing this actively again. Over the last six years, advanced ministerial degrees have been the fastest growing degree category for Canadian seminaries in ATS (ATS 2011–2012 Annual Data Tables 2.2 and 2.3). My major reservations about the DMin are, first of all, that it is a degree of unproven worth. What exactly can a person do with a DMin that the same person cannot do with another theological degree?

Some might say that they can teach in a theological institution, but I would question whether this is accurate, as the DMin was never designed as an academic degree (even if it is used this way). Hence, in many ways the DMin remains a "dead end" degree (to quote a person who should remain anonymous) if one wishes to keep educational options open regarding ministry and other avenues. It is entirely possible that a well-thought-out program of continuing education would better serve the purposes of pastors wishing for more theological knowledge. It waits to be seen whether this degree actually helps its institutions in the long term.

The second trend is the emphasis on advanced research degrees. The offering of advanced research degrees has also become an apparent strategy for ATS institutions, including Canadian ones. As with advanced ministerial degrees, advanced research degrees have also shown growth over the last six years (ATS 2011–2012 Annual Data Table 2.15). There are nine Canadian ATS institutions that emphasize advanced research degrees, two of them evangelical institutions. These include: Emmanuel College of Victoria University with 62 total students and 45 full-time equivalent in the MDiv, and 45 total students and 43 full-time equivalent in advanced research degrees; Lutheran Theological Seminary (SK), with 15/3 in the MDiv, and 5/3 in advanced research degrees; McGill University Faculty of Religious Studies with 32/32 in the MDiv, and 44/44 in advanced research degrees; McMaster Divinity College, with 55/38 in the MDiv, and 53/53 in advanced research degrees; Regis College, with 19/16 in the MDiv, and 57/41 in advanced research degrees; St. Paul University Faculty of Theology, with 0 MDiv students, and 30/30 in advanced research degrees; Trinity College Faculty of Divinity, with 33/18 in the MDiv, and 20/18 in advanced research degrees; University of St. Michael's College, with 12/9 in the MDiv, and 89/88 in advanced research degrees; and Wycliffe College, with 50/35 in the MDiv, and 61/58 in advanced research degrees. Whereas advanced research degrees have recognized academic integrity, and even the ability to help prepare people for ministerial work if structured appropriately, the major questions with this strategy are the cost of the degree within the institution and the need for trained academics in a world that seems to have less interest in theology. The running of advanced theological degree programs is institutionally quite expensive, as it requires specialized faculty, small class sizes, and other additional resources such as library and electronic resources—all of which can impose a disproportionately large financial burden on an institution, especially if it is struggling to survive. Further, if there are fewer people interested in Christianity—as reflected by static or decreasing church attendance and fewer interested in seminary itself—then it stands to reason that there will be fewer interested in studying it in other venues, and hence less need for trained academics to teach it.

There are many factors regarding curriculum to consider. These include the degrees offered, their content, their availability and access, and their means of delivery, among others. However, I believe that one of the inhibiting factors in theological education has been the lack of a spirit of adventure and innovation. There has been a genuine hesitance to try to develop new curricular offerings and degrees that address the kinds of situations that ministry of today requires. Instead, there has been an attempt to make the one old shoe fit all feet. This has been, I believe, one of the major shortcomings of ATS as an accrediting agency. We all know that accrediting agencies themselves are not meant to be innovators, but I believe that ATS has been particularly recalcitrant, placing the priorities of the mainstream Protestant institutions—even though they have represented smaller numbers of students for some time—ahead of those of the evangelical institutions. The result is emphasis upon a degree that is old-fashioned and out of date. It is only recently that ATS is addressing this issue with its latest revision of the standards, but I fear that it is too little and perhaps too late. There is still not enough innovative thinking and even the allowing of institutions to develop and pioneer new types of degree programs to ensure currency in their educational offerings. Another major shortcoming of ATS is that it is accredited by CHEA, an accrediting agency of accrediting agencies responsible to the United States Department of Education. The increasing intrusion of the Department of Education is bound to cost theological institutions both their freedom to operate and perhaps their finances to do so. For example, the latest edict is that future ATS accrediting visits will require a ministry practitioner on each panel, and for those with mediated learning programs expertise in this area. The costs of these additional people will be borne by the institutions themselves. This does not even address the advisability or practicality of adding such people, such as ministry practitioners with sufficient knowledge and expertise to participate in accreditation. Education (and its scrutiny and regulation) is not meant to be a federal governmental function in the United States, and so this clear case of constitutional violation can only have long-term detriments. To a large extent, this encroachment was exacerbated, if not brought on, by the United States guaranteed federal loan program, as colleges and universities in the United States became more and more dependent upon students getting federal loans as their tuition costs consistently outstripped inflation by sizeable amounts. As a result, it is perhaps time to weigh whether Canadians should consider establishing a separate accrediting agency for Canadian institutions of theological education. We can learn from the shortcomings of those in the United States by resisting the urge to over-bureaucratize the process and allow institutions to innovate and embrace the need for change.

*Implications for Practice*

Despite the situation I have identified, there are still some Canadian seminaries that are probably "indestructible." By indestructible, I mean that they will be able to survive for the next thirty to fifty years—although even here I believe that there are cautions for all of our institutions. I apologize if I am inaccurate in some of the observations that I make, but they are designed to glean implications from which all institutions can learn.

The first category of indestructible institution is the closely linked denominational seminary. In this category, for instance, is Canadian Southern Baptist Seminary in Cochrane, Alberta. On the basis of their ATS website, they have a number of issues that they must address, but they also have strong backing from the Southern Baptist mission board. As long as the mission board believes in the work of the seminary, they will probably survive, despite low enrollment, a budget that probably cannot be balanced on the basis of tuition, a small faculty, and other challenges. Similar is Wycliffe College in Toronto. With the problems that the Anglican Church of Canada is having, and comparison of Wycliffe to the other Anglican theological colleges, I am confident that the evangelicals within the Canadian Anglican church will ensure that Wycliffe remains viable. Wycliffe is also a member of the Toronto School of Theology. Membership helps to provide added resources, especially faculty, so that Wycliffe can afford to have a relatively small faculty and still continue to offer degrees, including advanced research degrees. However, there is the constant challenge of working with faculty who are not of the same theological convictions and institutions whose own priorities are very different. Apart from these two, I cannot see any other Canadian institutions that are so denominationally secure.

The second category of institution is endowment supported. In this category belongs my own institution, McMaster Divinity College, whose endowment has doubled over the last ten or so years. Having a relatively large endowment is a tremendous asset. As noted above, there are a number of restrictions that it entails, but it also provides a solid financial platform upon which to build. Even with the fluctuations in the market, with a wise and well-managed endowment one can endure such uncertainty and ensure that there is sufficient funding to continue. Such an endowment may provide for such an institution to survive, but it may also mean that it does not thrive, through over-dependence upon the endowment at the expense of developing other sources of income, such as annual donor giving and tuition revenue (our tuition rate is significantly lower than many institutions, and probably lower than it should be). However, if the situation became dire enough, with sufficient cutbacks in faculty and staff, McMaster Divinity College could probably weather most financial storms.

The final indestructible institution is Regent College in Vancouver, British Columbia. Regent has a reasonable endowment for an evangelical institution, but its strength is in its international profile, which allows it to attract students from all over the world. This includes not only Canada but the United States and abroad. Most seminaries remain strictly regional institutions. That is, they attract the vast majority of their students from their own immediate area. This is true for most seminary programs, except for advanced degrees, especially advanced research degrees. But for most master's level degrees, students attend institutions within their immediate area. Regent has overcome this limitation and so has expanded its catchment area probably beyond that of any other seminary in Canada, and certainly any other evangelical institution. Regent also has reasonably favorable tuition costs when its tuition costs are compared to those of its competitive institutions across North America. Compared to most other Canadian seminaries, however, Regent is relatively more expensive, which may imperil its future growth.

## *Suggestions for Further Consideration*

Three issues merit further consideration and research. The first is the overall educational and cultural situation in which Canadian seminaries, and in particular evangelical seminaries, find themselves. This research is only a first step. Most of our institutions are long-lived and continue to endure, despite fluctuating circumstances. The rate at which institutions die out is surprisingly slow, and so it takes some time for them to disappear. Nevertheless, disappear they do in one form or another. What I would wish for is something much more robust for all—that is, thriving seminaries that have sufficient and growing resources to be able to educate students the way that they deserve to be educated, money to pay faculty what they deserve to be paid, and buildings that are appropriate for the use to which they are put. In this light, Canadian theological education has serious challenges ahead of it that must be investigated. The two major challenges are student enrollment and finances, and these are inextricably related to each other. Sufficient students are required to offer the programs that are needed to generate the tuition revenue to sustain such institutions. Other means of finances are required to continue to build such institutions, whether long-term investments or yearly contributions.

The second issue is partnerships. Of all of the possible ways forward in addressing a challenging situation, partnerships have not emerged as a viable means of moving forward, and we need to know why. Good partnerships provide the opportunity for two or more institutions to work together in ways that economize on relatively scarce resources, while also allowing institutional identity to be retained. One apparently successful amalgamation by the Christian and Missionary Alliance and Church of the Nazarene created Ambrose University College in Calgary, Alberta. However, I do not know of a similar venture among seminaries or theological graduate schools in Canada. If I am right in my estimations and analyses above, all Canadian seminaries are going to face much more difficult times ahead before they face easier times, and so partnerships that would promote their work while also maintaining institutional identity and integrity would seem prudent. The ideal time for such partnerships is when institutions are relatively secure and sound, rather than waiting until one or more of them is in serious financial trouble and has thus curtailed its available options. At that point, it is probably too late for a constructive partnership. Nevertheless, The stakeholders in institutions often would apparently rather lose their institutions and all that they have accomplished and accumulated through the years than run the risk of partnering with an "unworthy" institution. The perception of such unworthiness is, in my experience, usually based upon relatively insignificant issues when compared with the losses that can be incurred by failure to take positive steps together.

Finally, I believe that the current situation of accreditation provides a useful opportunity to investigate whether a Canadian-wide evangelical accrediting agency for theological institutions might be wise. I do not see any immediate remedy to the situation in the United States with increasing governmental encroachment upon what was designed to be a voluntary and peer-regulated process that has now become a federalized, bureaucratized, and imposed structure, with decreasing freedom for accrediting agencies (who themselves must now be accredited) and their institutions. I am not suggesting that Canadians mirror what has happened in the United States but that we learn from what went wrong and investigate building a new and robust volunteer accrediting agency that is flexibly responsive to the needs of its member institutions. By this, we can guarantee all that we wish to guarantee about theological education, while providing leadership to others, both here and in the United States, regarding how such an agency and its institutions can function.

## Conclusion

In this paper, I have attempted to revisit five years later the situation regarding seminary education in Canada. I would have liked to report that the potential problems that I identified then have all been satisfactorily addressed, so that we face a clear and unhindered future for theological education at the seminary and graduate level in Canada. To the contrary, I believe that many of the problems that I identified are at least as severe, or even more dire, than they were when I addressed them those few short years ago. There is a clear crisis in student enrollment that all institutions must face and address together, because it has serious ramifications for our institutional existence. These are closely related to issues of finances upon which we are all dependent. I do not have any quick fixes to these problems, but I have suggested that there are some areas that we can pursue together to address such concerns, including enrollment and finances, constructive partnerships, and even new forms of accreditation. I am sure there are many more such proposals that merit discussion as well.

## Bibliography

Christensen, Clayton M., and Henry J. Eyring. *The Innovative University: Changing the DNA of Higher Education from the Inside Out*. San Francisco: Jossey-Bass, 2011.

Porter, Stanley E. "Theological Education in the Twenty-first Century." *Toronto Journal of Theology Supplement* 1 (2009) 41–54.

## The Cross and the Women of Galilee:
## A Feminist Theology of Salvation

Karyn Carlo

New York Theological Seminary, New York, NY, USA

> Many women were also there, looking on from a distance; they had followed Jesus from Galilee and had provided for him.
> — Matt 27:55 (NRSV)

### Introduction

The Christian faith was born in a time and place where people were crucified by the thousands. Jesus of Nazareth was one of them. In one sense, his cross was no different than all those other crosses and his suffering was no different than the suffering of any other crucified person. But, for centuries, Christianity has set his cross apart, claiming that Jesus was not only a human being but God incarnate and that the nature and purpose of his suffering was unique, either as a vicarious atonement for human sin made possible by one perfect sacrifice, as an extraordinary moral example of love and obedience to God, or as a cosmic victory over suffering and death. All of these ways of thinking about the cross—the classical atonement theories—have rich and meaningful histories and clearly speak to the nature of the faith. That is why they have been around for so long. But they also have their limitations. In each of these theories, the cross of Jesus of Nazareth, and what Jesus suffered there, seems disconnected from the many crosses of history where others have suffered, and continue to suffer, from the injustices in this world.

The particular social location of Jesus of Nazareth, an oppressed Jew living under Roman domination, is not part of any of these theologies. His cross is unrelated to the social and political reality of crucifixion, his suffering is different from the suffering of other crucified people, and the hope of his resurrection is for souls in eternity but not for bodies in this world. And yet, as evangelical Christians, we affirm a specifically *bodily* resurrection, not an abstraction. That means Jesus' cross, while unique, must also be connected to the many other crosses of history and his resurrection must be connected, not only to a hope for souls in the afterlife, but for bodies in this life as well.

Liberation theologians have made some inroads into making these theological connections. They insist that Jesus' identity as an impoverished and oppressed person, a Galilean Jew in the Roman Empire and subject to the punishment of crucifixion, is not only socially and historically important, but theologically significant as well. For them, the crucifixion and resurrection of Jesus signifies God's solidarity with the oppressed people of the world. The cross of Jesus of Nazareth is connected with the other crosses of that time and in his resurrection is the hope of a coming reign of God breaking into this world in concrete social, political, and economic terms. This is a significantly different point of view from that of earlier atonement theories, one that speaks to many people for whom the problem of the non-person in society and the salvation of bodies in this world is at least as important as the other-worldly, individual salvation of the soul. But it also has some limitations.

Even when the cross of Jesus is united with the crosses of history, and through it, God is understood to be in solidarity with oppressed people, the idea that we are saved solely by suffering is not experienced as good news by everybody. For example, victims of intimate violence often struggle to learn the lesson that love doesn't hurt. How does that square with the idea that the love of God is proved through the suffering of Christ? Is there another way of telling the story of the death and resurrection of Jesus that moves us beyond the limitations of a theology of redemptive suffering toward another way of thinking about the cross? I think that part of the answer can be found in the story of the lamentation and protest of the women of Galilee.

These women are depicted in all the Gospels as present at the crucifixion of Jesus and as the first to witness and proclaim his resurrection. While others in the Gospel stories, including most of the male disciples, move away from the cross, the women move toward it. These women act much like many women I have encountered as a police officer on the streets of New York who, at the scene of a shooting or another violent death, are often the first to want to cross police lines to minister to the body, to grieve, to cry out in deep protest, to refuse to "let another one be lost to the streets," and who act to make that so.

Viewed through the eyes of the women of Galilee, the cross and resurrection of Jesus are not primarily a moment for atonement through valorized suffering, or a call to exemplary obedience, a tale of a singularly heroic and victorious male savior, or a call to inappropriate self-abnegation. They reflect a tale of shared trauma and grief over an event that, like all crucifixions, should never have happened, and a "seeing of the Lord" that began in this community of women as they witnessed the power of God's love to literally raise the dead.

The story of the cross and the women of Galilee is the story of anyone who has encountered God's grace and resurrecting power in the midst of brutality and death. By including these women in our own understanding of the nature of Jesus' death and resurrection, we can come to see the cross, not only as a saving death or heroic sacrifice, but also as a place of lament and protest that opens our eyes to the power of bodily resurrection in our lives and in our communities as well. To understand this better, it is important to consider some of the historical context in which the Galilean women who first followed Jesus were living and some of the traditions that prevailed there.

### *Mourning Rituals in the First Century Jewish and Greco-Roman World*

Rituals of mourning were widespread in antiquity throughout the Greco-Roman and the Jewish world, and women were the primary participants. Their purpose was to affirm the worth of the life that was lost. Since having one's death go unmourned was thought of as a great disgrace, these rituals served to affirm the dignity of human life, often in the midst of brutal circumstances.

In the case of people killed by the state, rituals of lament could actually serve as a form of protest against execution. As Kathleen Corley puts it, "the powerful potential of funerals for complaint and protest through the mourning of women and kin is no doubt one reason why criminals and traitors were usually denied burial rites and mourning and their bodies either dumped into mass graves or simply left to rot unburied outside of city walls."[1]

In reference to the relationship between mourning and crucifixion, Corely writes,

> [E]xecutions were intended to provide a public display of Roman force to serve as a deterrent to dissent, and the proceedings were hardly intended to facilitate public mourning and normal burial practices. In view of the inherent potential for disruption posed by women's emotional lamentation of the dead this is not surprising.[2]

In fact, mourning was prohibited at crucifixions as evidenced in the *Gospel of Peter* 12:1–5 "although on the day the master was crucified we could not mourn or beat our breasts, now let us perform these rites at his tomb."

In other words, the lamentation of women served to disrupt the normalized violence of crucifixion and served as a protest against the oppression of the Roman Empire. Whereas the oppressors did everything they could to get the message across that those they crucified were nobodies, those who loved them, particularly the women, did everything they could to affirm their humanity. In this way, women from oppressed communities, such as that surrounding Jesus, engaged in a profound resistance to the dehumanizing violence of their oppressors, and refused to let the Roman Empire define the worth, value, and humanity of their people.

In addition to this tension between the officials of the Roman Empire and the relatives and loved ones of those they executed, there was also another gender-based tension. In the highly patriarchal context of the first century Jewish and Greco-Roman

---

1. Corley, *Women and the Historical Jesus*, 110–11.
2. Ibid., 118.

world, there was an enormous difference between the way women and men typically responded to death. Whereas women frequently grieved and lamented death and openly displayed their emotion, men praised the deceased and restrained all outward signs of feeling. This was done in the tradition of the *epitaphios logos* or funeral oration, in which praise, not mourning, served to valorize the lives of the dead, particularly in the case of men who died on behalf of the state.[3] These different reactions, conditioned by different gender roles, were not equally valued. As is usually the case in patriarchal society, the "men's way" of doing things was more highly valued and the "women's way" was denigrated. As Corley puts it,

> Women's mourning which focused on the pain of the loss and the continued connection with the loved one, became negatively coded, whereas male praise of the dead took on positive value. Male grief was characterized by restraint and praise for the dead, whereas women's mourning was considered 'uncontrolled' and 'unmanly' in spite of the apparent orderliness of their religious rites.[4]

I argue that though it is devalued, this "uncontrolled" and "unmanly" mourning in the face of unjust and violent death, exemplified by the story of the women of Galilee, is an important part of the way the early disciples came to understand the death and resurrection of Jesus.

## Galilean Women and the Jesus Movement

Galilee lay on the fringe of the Roman Empire. Since the sixth century BCE, it had been under the control of various foreign empires (Babylonian, Persian, Greco-Egyptian, Greco-Syrian, and Roman) and was currently ruled by Antipas, the son of Herod the Great. Historical and archeological evidence points toward Roman oppression of Galilee in several ways: (1) Roman imperial policy was an affront to the values of traditional Jewish religion,[5] (2) the commercialization and urbanization of Galilee,

3. Ibid., 110.
4. Ibid.
5. Crossan, *The Birth of Christianity*, 176.

made manifest in the building and rebuilding of Galilean cities for the benefit of the Roman Empire, led to an increase in the social and economic exploitation of Jewish peasants whose goods, labor, and taxes all went to support these projects,[6] and (3) the dominance of imperial Rome was maintained by violence, including crucifixions,[7] creating ongoing trauma in these communities.

Antipas rebuilt Sepphoris in 4 BCE[8] and founded the city of Tiberius in 19 CE, thus creating two major urban centers in Galilee. Far from contributing to people's well being, this building and rebuilding of cities by the Romans contributed to an increase in social inequality and an oppressive social and economic dynamic that was unfavorable to the Jewish peasants of the region, who were forced to support these cities with their labor, their goods, and their taxes. Not only was land, which traditional Jewish religion viewed as belonging only to God, treated as an "entrepreneurial commodity" by the Romans, development also happened in a way that destroyed the livelihood of the Jewish people.[9] This social and economic oppression was, of course, maintained by the presence of raw power and military force[10] including frequent and public crucifixions as a means of bringing conquered people and rebellious provinces under control.[11]

Unlike the traditional Jewish method of exposure mentioned in Deuteronomy, in which a person was "hung on a tree" after death as a public warning and removed by sunset, Roman crucifixion was particularly brutal, as well as humiliating to Jewish people, in that the victim was crucified alive and, most often, denied burial.[12] In that way, this practice served as an affront to the Jewish belief in the righteousness of God and

6. Ibid., 218–23.
7. Ibid., 543.
8. Reed, *Guide to the New Testament*, 54. No archeological evidence of damage at Sepphoris has been found. Therefore, New Testament scholarship is not united in this opinion, which is based on Josephus.
9. Ibid., 209.
10. Ibid., 231.
11. Hengel, *Crucifixion*, 46–47.
12. Ibid., 542.

social justice. It also served as a profound insult to their sense of human dignity.[13]

In addition to the social, economic, and political oppression of the Galilean people, there was also the reality of poverty, hunger, and disease. As was the case throughout the ancient world, both life and health in this region were fragile. The life expectancy was roughly twenty years, even lower for women who often died in childbirth.[14] As Reed puts it, "Life and health was, in Galilee and the whole ancient world, much more fragile than it is today. . . About every fourth birth resulted in a death, either of the mother or the child."[15]

This type of multi-layered oppression, quite understandably, engendered resistance and rebellion. In fact, although Galilee had been under foreign domination long before the dawn of the Roman Empire, there was much more resistance to the Romans than to any other oppressors. As Crossan puts it, "Within the first four hundred years of foreign control, under the Persian Empire and its Greek replacements, there was only a single revolt, at the very end of that period. But within the first two hundred years of Roman control there were three major revolts . . ."[16] As Richard Horsley puts it, "the Judeans and Galileans were perhaps the most adamant in reasserting their independence and defending their traditional way of life, persisting in their resistance for nearly two centuries before the Roman armies 'pacified' Palestine more permanently."[17]

These resistance movements took various forms, some overtly rebellious and others more subtle, offering a way for the people to hope for something other than the poverty, violence, and oppression they experienced in their lives. It was into this context that Jesus was born. No doubt there were many reasons why Galileans would be attracted to Jesus, the healer who spoke of another way of life—a countercultural kingdom God. But why

---

13. Hengel, *Crucifixion*, 87–88.
14. Reed, *Visual Guide*, 68.
15. Ibid., 69.
16. Crossan, *The Birth of Christianity*, 177.
17. Horsley, *Jesus and Empire*, 35.

would Galilean women be attracted to the movement? Perhaps it was, as Tal Ilan suggests, because "the power and authority Jesus claimed for himself derived not from the main bodies of power of his time . . . but rather from the charismatic fringes,"[18] those activities such as healing and prophecy that typically happened outside the usual institutions of authority such as the temple or the priesthood. According to Ilan,

> [W]omen could and did emerge from these fringes in similar capacities. Jesus is thus to be found in typical feminine settings and accused of typical feminine transgressions. His message, even when not entirely feminist in character, would be understood by women because he spoke in a familiar language and went through familiar motions.[19]

Elaine M. Wainwright makes a similar argument, claiming that healing was an essential connection between Jesus and women, one that united them in a nonhierarchical way. She writes, "The healer and the healed cannot be isolated from one another nor constructed hierarchically within the symbolic universe of early Christianity."[20] In other words, Jesus' healing ministry created a community in which women were included and treated as equals. Unfortunately, other than the fact that there *were* women in this movement, as evidenced by ample scriptural references to their presence,[21] and speculation such as that cited above concerning the reasons why Galilean women would have been attracted to Jesus, not much is known about them as individuals. Only a few women about whom little else is known are named in the Gospels. Many more go unnamed. The only exception to this is Mary Magdalene.

---

18. Ilan, "Footsteps of Jesus," 117.
19. Ibid., 135.
20. Wainwright, "Your Faith," 243.
21. See the list of women in Luke 8:1–3; the depiction of women as present at the cross in Mark 15:40–41; and in the "Empty tomb narratives" found in Matthew 27, Mark 16, Luke 24, and John 20 as well as numerous stories in the Gospels in which women were the recipients of Jesus' healing.

## Mary Magdalene

Very little is known even about Mary Magdalene as a historic figure. Her name suggests that she came from the city known in Aramaic as Magdala or Magadan (Migdal in Hebrew, which means "tower") a small city located by the Sea of Galilee by the base of Mount Arbel, noted for its trade in salted fish. According to the Gospels of Mark and Luke, Mary was delivered by Jesus from seven demons.[22] There are different ways of thinking about this exorcism. For example, Bruce Chilton sees it is a symbolic way of saying she was particularly liberated of evil and "uncleanness."[23] Corley, on the other hand, claims these exorcisms may be a reference to the way in which women who spent much time in tombs as part of their ritual lamentation were thought sometimes to be possessed by demons.[24] Either way, Mary is heavily associated with the healing ritual of exorcism, as well as lamentation, particularly in reference to the death of Jesus.

Although she is not mentioned in any of Paul's letters, in the Gospels of Matthew, Mark, and John, Mary Magdalene is depicted as the first to witness the risen Christ. While in these Gospels the male disciples are portrayed as having betrayed Jesus (Judas), denied Jesus (Peter) or simply hiding out in fear (the other disciples), she and the other women of Galilee are variously depicted as present at the crucifixion and as rising on the third day to minister to Jesus' crucified body. Although the entire process of crucifixion was designed by the Romans to dehumanize victims like Jesus and convince others of the worthlessness of their lives, these women, led by Mary Magdalene, were determined to affirm Jesus' dignity and the value of his life and ministry.

Mary's testimony, "I have seen the Lord"[25] (arguably the first Christian sermon!) still inspires people today, who are faced with dehumanizing violence and oppression and who long to know

---

22. Mark 16:9; Luke 8:2.
23. Chilton *Mary Magdalene*, 25–28.
24. Corley, *Women and the Historical Jesus*, 34.
25. John 20:18.

that God really did raise Jesus from the dead and there is, therefore, hope for us all. For example, consider Barbara Reid's experience in Peru, where women who had endured the loss of family members to the "Shining Path" movement turned to Mary Magdalene's story for courage and inspiration. Some of their words are as follows:

> When I lived in the selva, I was always silent when I saw injustices; now I have changed. I have become strong. If I see something that is wrong I speak out the truth about it. Like Mary Magdalene who turns around when she experienced the risen Christ, I have turned around. It's not easy to change and leave behind what was before.
> — Gloria [26]

> How can we follow Mary Magdalene's example and preach the good news? We have to throw off the old garments of anything that holds women back. And when you are on this mission, it feeds you and you learn. You speak differently, as you gain courage to go about preaching.
> — Adriana[27]

## *What Is Resurrection?*

But what exactly did Mary Magdalene and the other women of Galilee see and experience that gave them the courage to "go about preaching?" We are living in a time when nearly two millennia of Christian experience are behind us, during which we have given great consideration and engaged in no small amount of debate about the nature of the resurrection and what it means. This was not the case in the first century. There was no formal theology of the cross and resurrection, only strange encounters with the risen Lord that, even now, are hard to fully understand based upon human reason and logic.

Following the death of Jesus, his community was traumatized. Elizabeth Schüssler-Fiorenza tells us that:

---

26. Reid, *Taking up the Cross*, 113.
27. Ibid., 115.

> The early attempts of meaning-making in the face of the devastating execution of Jesus should not be conceptualized merely in terms of the history of ideas. Nor should they be understood primarily as responses to and affirmations of Jesus' resurrection. Rather, we must read these early Christian attempts of theological meaning-making as critical arguments that begin with the very real experience of Jesus' dehumanization and crucifixion as a political criminal.[28]

In other words, long before there was a Christian experience or theology of resurrection (let alone a sense of Christian triumphalism) there was an oppressed community traumatized by yet another brutal death. As was usually the case in the ancient Jewish and Greco-Roman world, it was likely that the male disciples responded to this death by eulogizing Jesus as a hero who died nobly while the female disciples responded with mourning rituals that emphasized the pain of loss. Both of these responses to violent and de-humanizing death are present in the Gospels.

On the surface, the Gospels tend to valorize the male response to the death of Jesus over that of women. Even while adopting the funerary traditions and mourning rituals of women as a source, the presumably male Gospel writers tended to use these stories in service of narratives that stressed heroic death and noble sacrifice, not lamentation or loss. Nevertheless, if we read against the grain, the voices of women are still present, perhaps because they were simply too strong to silence entirely. These voices speak of grief and pain. They are the voices of lament, not eulogy.

In their story, the body matters. Resurrection is not a disembodied "spiritual" event unrelated to concrete human need in the here and now. The resurrected Jesus is described in the Gospels as embodied. He has flesh and blood and physical wounds,[29] and he eats fish for breakfast.[30] But there is something about the nature of his bodily presence that still speaks to mystery and transcendence. He walks through locked

---

28. Schüssler-Fiorenza, *Jesus*, 120.
29. Luke 24:39.
30. Luke 24:42; John 21:12–13.

doors[31] and is only recognized by believers (even then with difficulty). In fact, at first, the testimony of the Galilean women is not even believed by Jesus' own followers.[32] In short, the resurrection is not simply resuscitation, like that of Lazarus. It is both objective and subjective. That is, it is both embodied and recognizable and, at the same time, something mysterious and transcendent that can only be seen through the eyes of faith. According to the Gospel accounts, it also seems that the ability to "see the Lord" is, in great part, about the nature of the relationship people have with God and one another.

That is where the story of the Galilean women is useful. They encounter Jesus while in the midst of lament and protest, stemming from their great love for him, for one another, and for their oppressed community. There is a connection between such lament and protest and the ability to see the risen Christ. As Marianne Sawicki puts it,

> The women at the tomb were observing the customs of mourning. They were weeping for Jesus. Their eyes were full of tears when the realization hit them that Jesus was not in the grave. For the poor, for widows, for a colonized nation, the eyes are the organs that register pain . . . They "saw" Jesus through their tears . . . Sixty years afterwards the churches had four sanitized little stories about a trip to a garden and a lovely surprise. But it wasn't like that when it happened. Grief may also be a precondition for resurrection, and tears for permitting the eyes to see.[33]

The women of Galilee "saw the Lord" and so can we. Just as Jesus was present to them, Jesus can also be present to us, as we are present to one another and as we struggle for justice and love in our world. Part of what it means to be present to one another involves shared lamentation. Mourning rituals are essential to the life of a community, creating a sense of continuity and ongoing connection between the living and the dead. Funerary rituals, particularly those involving meals shared with the dead, in which their presence is invoked and celebrated, were very important to

---

31. John 20:19, 26.
32. Mark 16:13.
33. Sawicki, *Seeing the Lord*, 92–93.

the early Christian community as one way of coping with the ongoing trauma of violent death. As Corley puts it:

> These funerary rituals are what create community, by solidifying the relationship between the living members of the community, and by connecting them with the deceased of the community. There is connection, there is presence, both of the living and the dead. We will see that it is women who were the primary actors in these funerary rituals and meals which were so important to the communal lives of the earliest Christian groups, and therefore it is the women who generated the central elements that created the Christian community: memorial meals for the dead Jesus, the Passion narrative which memorialized Jesus' death in narrative form, as was the notion that the dead Jesus was "raised and appeared" in the midst of the community in their memorial meals and rituals through the lament of ancient Christian women.[34]

In other words, Corey thinks that both what she terms the "Eucharist," as well as the Passion narratives, including the Empty Tomb stories, began, not as a tradition of noble death or heroic sacrifice, but as woman-led funerary rituals, quite common in the larger Jewish and Greco-Roman world, in which, in the midst of mourning, the ongoing presence of the dead is experienced and affirmed.

Reflecting on their own pastoral experience of healing, Rita Nakashima Brock and Rebecca Parker tell us that "held in the embrace of a community's rituals and traditions, grief can find its depth, anger can voice its anguish and protest can fuel creative action that holds out the possibilities of restored and protected life even in the midst or the aftermath of injustice and tragedy."[35] That is my vision for the church today, a place where life can be affirmed and protected, even in the midst of a violent world. That is where the impact and significance of Jesus' resurrection can be mostly deeply felt.

Not long before her own death, Mamie Till-Mobley, the mother of Emmet Till, who was lynched at the age of 14, said,

---

34. Corley, *Maranatha*, 17.
35. Brock and Parker, *Saving Paradise*, 407.

> [M]y story is more than a story of a lynching. It is more than a story of how, with God's guidance, I made a commitment to rip the covers off Mississippi, USA—revealing to the world the horrible face of race hatred . . . It is the story of how I was able to pull myself back from the brink of desolation and turn my life around by digging deep within my soul to pull hope from despair, joy from anguish, forgiveness from anger, love from hate.[36]

This is what resurrection looks like, the ongoing reality of life renewed and restored despite everything that opposes it. This is where the cross of Jesus of Nazareth intersects with the crosses of history and brings us new hope, not only for souls for eternity, but for bodies here in this world. Because Jesus was raised bodily from the dead, we can experience renewed life, not only "there and then" in eternity but "here and now" as part of our embodied, earthly lives.

There are three ways in which this renewed life may happen. First, it can happen as the bodily salvation of those whose lives are spared by creative protest against violence. This was seen in the anti-lynching movements of the nineteenth and twentieth century as well as the ongoing protests against police brutality, street violence, and intimate violence that continue today. By disrupting, lamenting, and protesting such violence, those who act help spare more people from similar needless suffering. Unlike theologies of the cross that focus only on the individual salvation of the soul in eternity, what I am proposing includes the collective salvation of bodies in this world as well as an important dimension of the renewed life of resurrection.

Second, there is the resurrection of life's purpose. Those who grieve lives lost to violence can at least feel like their loved ones have "not died in vain." Although their involuntary suffering and death was not redemptive, something good can still come out of the situation. Families and loved ones of murder victims, and all who care about them, need this kind of resurrection. In fact this determination not to let a loved one "die in vain" often gives rise to action in the world that saves bodies as well, uniting this second dimension of resurrection with the first. People who

---

36. Till-Mobley and Bensen, *Death of Innocence*, xxiii.

grieve more "ordinary" loss need this resurrection of purpose, for even the powerful and privileged die, sometimes quite horribly. Their loved ones need space to mourn as well. There are many crosses in the world and many forms of resurrection. Because Jesus died as a victim of crucifixion, a theology of the cross must begin with that type of suffering and death as a starting point. But it does not end there. By turning away from theologies of the cross that normalize or justify violence and move toward lamentation and protest of unjust suffering and death, we find that there is a place at the cross for mourning other forms of loss as well.

Finally, resurrection is the healing that happens in the lives of bereaved people when the depths of grief—what Till-Mobley describes as the "deep digging in my soul"—give way to hope, joy, forgiveness, and love. It is the affirmation of life against all odds, of which Kadiatou Diallo speaks when she says, "if there is anything as cruel as the taking of a man's life, it is the taking away of his story, the particulars that make him holy. The mother who dreams that she can undo any harm that comes to her child, dreams fruitlessly. The one last thing she can do is to try to give her child back his story, the greatest and least obligation she can fulfill."[37] In the redemptive lamentation and protest of the women of Galilee there is this deep digging in the soul, giving way to an experience of resurrection that is the beginning of the hope of God's eternal life.

## Bibliography

Brock, Rita Nakashima, and Rebecca Parker. *Saving Paradise: How Christianity Traded Love of This World for Crucifixion and Empire*. Boston: Beacon, 2008.

Chilton, Bruce. *Mary Magdalene: A Biography*. New York: Doubleday, 2005.

---

37. Diallo and Wolf, *My Heart Will Cross This Ocean*, v.

Corley, Kathleen E. *Maranatha: Funerary Meals, Lament, Women and Christian Origins*. Minneapolis: Fortress, 2010.

———. *Women and the Historical Jesus: Feminist Myths of Christian Origins*. Santa Rosa, CA: Polebridge, 2002.

Crossan, John Dominic. *The Birth of Christianity: Discovering What Happened in the Years Immediately Following the Execution of Jesus*. New York: HarperCollins, 1998.

Diallo, Kadiatou, and Craig Wolf. *My Heart Will Cross This Ocean: My Story, My Son, Amadou*. New York: Ballantine, 2004.

Hengel, Martin. *Crucifixion in the Ancient World and the Folly of the Message of the Cross*. Translated by John Bowden. Minneapolis: Fortress, 1977.

Horsley, Richard A. *Jesus and Empire: The Kingdom of God and the New World Disorder*. Minneapolis: Fortress, 2003.

Ilan, Tal. "In the Footsteps of Jesus." In *Transformative Encounters: Jesus and Women Re-viewed*, edited by Ingrid R. Kitzberger, 115–36. BIS 43. Leiden: Brill, 1999.

Reed, Jonathan L. *The HarperCollins Visual Guide to the New Testament: What Archeology Reveals about the First Christians*. New York: HarperCollins, 2007.

Reid, Barbara E. *Taking up the Cross: New Testament Interpretations through Latina and Feminist Eyes*. Minneapolis: Fortress, 2007.

Sawicki, Marianne. *Seeing the Lord: Resurrection and Early Christian Practice*. Minneapolis: Fortress, 1994.

Schüssler-Fiorenza, Elisabeth. *Jesus: Miriam's Child, Sophia's Prophet, Critical Issues in Feminist Christology*. London: Continuum, 1994.

Till-Mobley, Mamie, and Christopher Bensen. *Death of Innocence: The Story of the Hate Crime that Changed America*. New York: Ballantine, 2004.

Wainwright, Elaine M. "Your Faith Has Made You Well." In *Transformative Encounters: Jesus and Women Re-viewed*, edited by Ingrid R. Kitzberger, 224–44. BIS 43. Leiden: Brill, 1999.

## NATURE LANGUAGE IN ISAIAH 1–39 AND ITS IMPLICATIONS FOR ENVIRONMENTAL ETHICS: INTERACTING WITH HILARY MARLOW'S *BIBLICAL PROPHETS AND CONTEMPORARY ENVIRONMENTAL ETHICS*

William R. Osborne
College of the Ozarks, Point Lookout, MO, USA

The relationship between human beings and the natural world is one of the weightiest matters facing contemporary politics, ethics, and religion. Recent studies purporting global climate change—with all of its supposed anthropogenic effects—have prompted a popular debate that is often won on account of volume, not veracity. However, *ad hominem* attacks do not move the discussion forward for either side. In order for Christians to speak into the public arena intelligibly and truthfully, a biblical position on such environmental concerns must be established. Developing a biblical position demands careful study of biblical texts, and Hilary Marlow, Lecturer in Hebrew and Old Testament at the University of Cambridge and Associate of the Faraday Institute for Science and Religion, has sought to provide such research in her recent work *Biblical Prophets and Contemporary Environmental Ethics*. In this volume, Marlow focuses specifically upon three eighth-century prophets and their perspective on the natural world. The following passage identifies both the direction and methodology of her research:

> [W]hat insights might a close study of the biblical texts yield, and is there a viable ecological hermeneutic to be derived from such readings? What principles derived from the text might inform discussions in environmental ethics, and conversely, how might the issues faced today influence reading of the texts? The aim of this book is to use the tools of biblical studies to provide an in-depth exegesis of part of

the Old Testament, namely some of the prophetic books, to answer such questions.[1]

In the earlier part of the book, Marlow offers a historical survey of the relationship between Christianity and the environment, arguing that the Christian worldview throughout much of church history helped produce "the industrial and technological materialism of today with its negative environmental impacts."[2] Marlow concludes the study by asserting that her reading of the text demonstrates that such a utilitarian anthropocentric view of the natural world cannot be derived from Amos, Hosea, or Isaiah 1–39. The biblical data, according to Marlow, present a worldview that sees humanity as closely interrelated with God, the natural world, and other human beings. Therefore, any appropriate and environmentally ethical reading of the text must take into account this triangular pattern of relationships among God, humanity, and non-human creation (i.e., "nature"). Marlow's conclusions rely greatly upon her study of Isaiah 1–39. The intent of this article is to examine and evaluate the validity of Marlow's position, focusing specifically on her exegetical methodology and her treatment of nature language and imagery in Isaiah 1–39, along with its implications for environmental ethics.

Marlow prepares the way for her discussion of the biblical text by evaluating the exegetical methods developed in recent studies associated with ecological hermeneutics. She focuses upon the work of Norman Habel, founder of the Earth Bible Project (EBP)—a group devoted to ecologically sensitive readings of the Bible. Habel's ecological hermeneutic resembles liberation and feminist readings in that "For Habel, the assumption that the text, as well as most of its interpreters, is anthropocentric legitimizes adopting a hermeneutic of suspicion," which reads the text standing on the side of the oppressed, in this case nature.[3] In response, Marlow offers five substantial critiques of the EBP: (1) the systematic hermeneutical method adopted by the EBP (a reader-response approach) is too restrictive and does

1. Marlow, *Biblical Prophets*, 5–6.
2. Ibid., 81.
3. Ibid., 87.

not allow the text to speak for itself, (2) the touted connections between ecological and feminist readings are superficial and not legitimate, (3) the terminology espoused by the group is imprecise and careless, (4) the eco-justice principles for interpretation set forth are more ideological than methodological, and (5) these same principles are secular in nature and are inappropriate for dealing with religious texts like the Bible. Marlow then seeks to develop and demonstrate an alternative approach to reading the Bible that is less anachronistic but no less relevant to contemporary environmental ethics.

She proposes the following "ecological triangle" as an alternative hermeneutic: God, Non-human creation, and Humanity. Approaching the Bible with this triangular paradigm, Marlow seeks to ask three questions of the text: (1) what understanding does the text present of non-human creation (local or cosmic)? (2) What are the assumptions of the author about Yahweh's relationship to the created world? And, (3) what effects do human actions have upon non-human creation and vice versa? Marlow stresses that such a methodology serves only as a background to her exegesis and is not a "formal grid" through which she interprets the text.

In her chapter "The Vineyard of the Lord of Hosts: YHWH, the People and the Land in Isaiah 1–39," Marlow employs her above methodology in exegetically studying passages referring to the natural world in Isaiah 1–39. She first addresses nature language in the context of cosmic imagery in Isa 14:12–15; 13:9–13; 34:2–5; and 24:1–13. Marlow's discussion of the first three texts is brief and consists mainly of a commentary that highlights the cause and effect relationship between the sin of human beings and its consequent cosmic effects to be rendered on the Day of Judgment. She writes: "YHWH clearly executes judgment on human behavior (13:9, 11; 34:2–3), and the effect in the heavens is portrayed as a reflection of this (13:10; 34:4). The heavens are not punished by YHWH for the sins of the people, but his anger disrupts the whole world order."[4]

---

4. Ibid., 199.

Marlow's treatment of Isaiah 24 is more substantial. She argues that this chapter represents a later redaction, and consequently, illustrates how "a message originally directed at the people of Israel is reconstructed to encompass the whole world and a powerful Israelite concept concerning the well-being of the land is universalized."[5] The principle of the text remains the same, according to Marlow, regardless of whether the text was written to address a local famine, a national disaster, or eschatological realities. Recognizing the thematic connections with Deuteronomy 28, Marlow asserts that the Isaiah text follows the basic framework of blessings and curses observed in the Pentateuch. Her emphasis is again fixed upon the cause and effect relationship exhibited by Israel's covenant disobedience and the languishing of the land that ensued.

Marlow redirects her study from cosmic language in Isaiah to the more common occurrence of nature language reflecting local flora and fauna. She first examines Isa 1:2–3 and 28:23–29, arguing that both texts are examples of the prophet appealing to the natural order in a way that makes nature Israel's exemplar. She posits that Isa 1:3, which compares Israel's disobedience to the obedience of an ox and a donkey, is a moral comparison. The contrast is "not between supposedly intelligent human beings and senseless beasts, but rather between those of God's creatures who act according to their God-given instincts and those who deliberately shun the divinely instituted moral order."[6] Similarly, the passage in Isaiah 28, according to Marlow, compares the wisdom of Yahweh in both agriculture and international relations. Verses 14–22 call Israel to trust in the Lord instead of Assyria, and verses 23–29 serve as an illustration of Yahweh's faithfulness to his people by giving good practices for farming. Marlow believes the passage to be a parable instructing Israelites to live in the world in harmony with their Creator and his established principles for interacting with the natural world.

Isaiah 1–39 includes more references to vines and viticulture than any other prophetic literature in the Old Testament, and

---

5. Ibid., 201.
6. Ibid., 209.

Marlow believes this to be significant to the writer's understanding of the natural world. Vine imagery in Isaiah is largely metonymic in that "Just as fruitful vines epitomize the blessings of YHWH, so too the presence of thorns and briers denotes removal of those blessings."[7] Devoting several pages to Isa 5:1–7 and 27:2–6, Marlow discusses the theological significance of the vine in Israel's self-perception as Yahweh's people and the prophet's depiction of Israel's future hope and judgment.

Continuing her study, Marlow examines Isaiah 34 and 35 and the relationship between humanity and animal populations communicated therein. These chapters present an antithetical picture of judgment and salvation with opposite effects reflected in the surrounding natural environments. Chapter 34 describes the desolation of Edom at the judgment of the Lord. Marlow comments on the de-creation motif created by the use of תהו (*tohu*, "formless") and בהו (*bohu*, "empty"), two parallel terms used in Gen 1:2 to describe pre-creation existence. She also notes that the scenario presented in Isaiah 34 is described by events not unfamiliar to modern ecology, such as: burning of the land and degradation of the soil (v. 9), desertification and depopulation (v. 10), encroachment of vegetation (v.13), species colonization (vv. 13, 14), and permanent habitat change (vv. 16, 17). The wild animals' permanent residence in the city is significant to Marlow. She writes: "It is only for the human population, not the animal one, that the outcome is disastrous."[8] The resulting picture of judgment does not portray the "wilderness" as inherently negative, or threatening to humanity, only out of place with respect to the divine order established in creation. The chapter refers to several different animals that are involved in the takeover of Edom. However, Marlow acknowledges that it is nearly impossible to determine with certainty which "wild" animals the text is referring to, due to the ambiguity of the Hebrew.

Isaiah 35, with its vision of restoration and regrowth, stands in stark contrast to chapter 34. The desert will be transformed by

---

7. Ibid., 209.
8. Ibid., 229.

life-giving water and the human population will receive divine healing at the coming of the glory of the Lord (v. 2). Similar realities are portrayed in Isa 11:1–10 as the "shoot of Jesse" reigns in righteousness and justice. In this passage the whole created order appears to be reversed, according to Marlow. The harmony created between wild and domestic animals, as well as with human beings, forms a new paradigm for the created world that transcends observable laws of nature. Marlow comments, "This depiction of perfection is not intended to negate the natural biological processes of the world, but rather to paint a wide picture of the potentiality of YHWH's ideal reign."[9] This picture of the ideal reign uses poetic and hyperbolic nature language in order to depict the radical change Yahweh will initiate in all creation.

Marlow develops her work by reflecting on her exegetical study and seeking to bridge the gap between the context of the ancient world and contemporary environmental concerns. She puts forward three "seminal ideas" that she believes help facilitate the dialogue between the two horizons of the Bible and the modern reader: (1) the value of non-human creation, (2) the ethics of human behavior, and (3) individual and community approaches. In describing the prophets' perceived value of non-human creation, she stresses her conclusion about the interconnectedness between humanity and the natural world. She writes: "The knowledge that human behaviour impacts other parts of creation, and vice versa, and the presupposition that this is part of the moral order of the universe form a fundamental part of the prophetic message."[10] Marlow argues that Isaiah's appeal to the natural world (e.g., Isa 1:2–3) and his portrayal of the earth as "mourning" (Isa 24:4), demonstrate a prophetic worldview that perceived non-human creation as having a separate identity and an inherent positive value. Marlow concedes that, at first glance, Isaiah appears to maintain a highly anthropocentric understanding of the natural world, but she argues that this is not a utilitarian anthropocentrism bent toward exploitation. She

9. Ibid., 241–42.
10. Ibid., 263.

develops her case as follows: (1) the sheer number of references to wild species in Isaiah suggests that observation of wildlife outside the city was part of daily life, (2) the idea of the "wilderness," or "wild," is ambiguous and cannot simply be interpreted to mean "hostile," and (3) Isa 34:14–17 describes the divine initiative to provide long-term rest and fecundity for wild animals, demonstrating that, at least in this case, human needs are not of primary concern.

Concluding her study, Marlow correlates her tripartite hermeneutic with her three ideas for bridging the culture gap. The result is a "new model" for reading texts that is anthropocentric (i.e., it begins with the interpreter's perceptions) and takes into account humanity's relationships to God, the natural world, and other human beings. Marlow summarizes her approach stating: "The model draws upon the principle of interconnectivity—which itself forms the basis both for science of ecology and for the worldview of the prophetic texts studied."[11] Interconnectivity between humanity and non-human creation is the central component of Marlow's study and proves to be the most demonstrable conclusion from her exegetical study.

Marlow's research is to be highly commended in at least two primary ways. First, her treatment and critiques of the EBP are fair and insightful. Her willingness to question the assumptions and hermeneutical presuppositions of people on her side of the global-warming debate reflects an interest in the biblical text over against environmental party lines. In fact, Marlow's work has potential to offend readers on either side of the debate, leaving her in an unpopular medial position. Her academic courage is laudable, and her commitment to productively move the discussion forward among Christians is greatly appreciated.

Marlow's conclusion that humanity is interconnected with non-human creation is biblically viable and well argued; indeed, it is perhaps the greatest contribution of the work. It is difficult to imagine an environmental position that would disagree with such a fundamental claim; however, Marlow's work presents a

---

11. Ibid., 275.

compelling case that Isaiah perceived the future of humanity and the future of the natural world as interconnected.

Marlow's exegesis of the Hebrew text in Isaiah is well done. She interacts with the text at a scholarly level often addressing significant matters such as compositional history, variant readings, and theological significance. Her interactions with other major commentators and authors, along with her attention to detail in exegesis, reveal her desire to engage the topic in a scholarly manner trying to allow the text to speak for itself.

Unfortunately, however, the present work also has several weaknesses that hinder the overall persuasiveness of the study. First, Marlow's foundational idea of interconnectivity between humanity and the natural world does not speak against utilitarian anthropocentrism in Isaiah, a position she argues is unbiblical. Marlow posits the ideas of interconnectivity and utilitarianism as if they are two mutually exclusive ways of viewing humanity's relationship with nature, but they simply are not. Proving the existence of interconnectivity, which Marlow does well, does not determine the grounds for the relationship—it only proves that one exists. It is quite possible to hold a utilitarian view toward the natural world, while believing there is a close interconnection between human beings and non-human creation. Marlow's negative understanding of utilitarianism appears to stem from her view that utilitarianism is synonymous with exploitation. Unfortunately, such loaded semantic associations could stifle Marlow's dialogue with Christians who believe that humanity can appropriately "use" the natural world but do not support the exploitation of it. It is ironic that Marlow criticizes the EBP for their carelessness and imprecision in language. Marlow's study, along with her conclusions, would have been greatly aided by a formal presentation of what she means by "utilitarian," especially since she is trying to argue for an anthropocentrism that is expressly not utilitarian.

Second, the cause and effect relationship highlighted in Isaiah strongly supports an anthropocentric view of nature that does not appear to place humanity and non-human creation on equal ground. In all of the examples provided of cause and effect in Isaiah 1–39, humanity and God are the cause while the natural world is the arena in which the effects are displayed. Such a one-sided cause and effect relationship points toward anthropocentrism or theocentrism in Isaiah's understanding of the natural world. In the quotation mentioned above, Marlow writes that a key part of Isaiah's message was "the knowledge that human behavior impacts other parts of creation, and vice versa."[12] However, the "vice versa" is not at all explicit in the text. Marlow provides no example (nor do I know of one) where the natural world is the cause and the effects are played out in humanity. Instead, the non-human creation passively reflects either the sinfulness of humanity or the glory of God depending upon the particular text and its redemptive-historical context. Within Isaiah 1–39, the espoused cause and effect relationship between humanity and non-human creation is not reciprocal. This is not to deny the reality that occurrences in the world, such as floods or famines, affect humanity, only that such a cause and effect relationship does not appear to be the concern of Isaiah.

Another weakness of Marlow's study is her belief that the concept of wilderness is not always a negative one in Isaiah. This position is superficial and not reflected by the text. Her claim that "The sheer number of wild species named [in Isaiah] suggests that observation of the landscape outside the city formed a part of daily life,"[13] is somewhat provocative, especially provided her own concession that scholarship can hardly determine what animals are being spoken of in much of Isaiah's prophetic menagerie (cf. Isaiah 34). Marlow seems to believe that the prophet's proximity to the natural world necessitates a benevolent view toward nature. She writes: "a part of Israelite community life is involved with, and dependent on the wild."[14] However, the people's dependence on the wild tends to support a utilitarian view of nature and does not necessitate a thoroughgoing positive perception of the natural world by the ancient Israelites.[15] Frequently in Isaiah, "wilderness" or that which is

---

12. Ibid., 263.
13. Ibid., 273.
14. Ibid.
15. Borowski, *Agriculture in Iron Age Israel*, 10.

"wild" is depicted as a means of judgment upon the people. In Isa 34:13 thorns and briars overtake buildings as a sign of judgment, and in Isa 35:9, the lack of lions and other beasts is a sign of restored creation. Other passages in Isaiah 1–39 describe the wilderness as negative using terms such as "a terrible land" (Isa 21:1) and "deserted and forsaken" (Isa 27:10). A positive or neutral understanding of the wild in Isaiah 1–39 is only derived from reading against the plain meaning of the literature.

Along similar lines, Marlow's exegesis of Isa 1:2–3 appears to reflect a vested interest in presenting the natural world as a highly valued "moral example" to humanity. Her interpretation of the text rejects the idea that the passage reflects a comparison between the intellect and rationality of animals over against that of human beings, even though the emphasis of the text is "knowledge" (ידע, *yada*), a word that has much more to do with understanding than moral uprightness. The passage seems to present an argument built upon the different mental capabilities of beasts of burden and human beings, and the case can be made that Isaiah is using a technique of argumentation that moves from "light to heavy," a strategy known in later Judaism as *qal vahomer*. The prophet begins with what is "light"—the manifested "knowledge" of non-rational animals in getting food from their owner—and then compares it to what is "heavy"—people who are far superior in intellect but lack knowledge of and provision from the Lord. It is also important to note that the animals, both known for stubbornness and difficulty in handling, are described in parallel with Israel's rebelliousness as a son. Therefore, it is possible that the text could point to both the ignorance and obstinacy of the animals, which, Isaiah asserts, Israel managed to surpass. Brevard Childs highlights the wisdom-like nature of these opening verses: "The accusation is made . . . in a parabolic form of wisdom. Israel has less understanding of its Lord than even the most stupid of domesticated animals."[16] The proposed alternative of interpreting Isa 1:3 as *qal vahomer* fits well in a parabolic context. Consequently, the weakness of Marlow's exegesis is that Isaiah's argument follows a progression

---

16. Childs, *Isaiah*, 17. See also Wildberger, *Isaiah 1–12*, 15.

and only works if there is an assumed qualitative difference between the two subjects being compared.

Next, Marlow derives most of her support for her arguments from Isaiah's agrarian context rather than explicit utterances recorded in the Bible, and at this point the question must be asked, is Marlow arguing for agrarianism over against urban culture? Is one more ethically right than the other? This factor of Marlow's research greatly reduces the effectiveness of her exegesis in defending her position, and demonstrates why her helpful treatment of the text offers little direction to her conclusions. If Isaiah's use of nature language and imagery simply flows from his agrarian context and immersion in the natural world, why should we conclude that such language holds any special meaning for the prophet? What other perception of the world did he have to draw upon in communicating to his audience? Marlow does not speak directly to the challenges of ethically and hermeneutically moving from an agrarian society to an urban one in her reading of Isaiah. When she does offer a brief comment, it is to state that her conclusions regarding ancient perceptions toward the natural world run counter to those found in scholarly literature on agrarianism in ancient Israel.[17] Provided that her presentation of the subject disagrees with modern scholarship, Marlow's argument would have been greatly strengthened by interacting with studies of extra-biblical materials that argue for a utilitarian and agrarian worldview in the ancient world. Along similar lines, a noteworthy absence is found in Marlow's failure to mention Ellen Davis's *Scripture, Culture, and Agriculture*, a monograph directly relating to an agrarian reading of Isaiah.

One final criticism can be brought against Marlow on account of her methodology. While she appropriately acknowledges the significance of the biblical data in articulating a contemporary Christian ethic on environmental issues, she appears to have arrived at her conclusions before examining the biblical text. In an earlier chapter she states that she will approach the text by an ecological hermeneutic that presupposes interconnectedness between God, humanity, and the natural world. She then con-

---

17. See Marlow, *Biblical Prophets*, 265.

cludes that her exegesis has proved that such close relationships exist. Could it be that what she found in biblical data was her own reflection? Given the fact that her survey of the biblical text does not cohere with, nor strongly support, her conclusions, the reader is left wondering which came first, the conclusions or the study?

The question remains whether or not Marlow's work will be accepted by the Christian audience to whom she is seeking to appeal. Her serious treatment of the biblical text will certainly attract the interest of many evangelical Christians who hold the Bible in high regard.

However, provided the aforementioned weaknesses, it would be a surprise if Marlow's research catapults the discussion to new heights. More radical environmentalists will likely take issue with Marlow's reluctant concession that the biblical data portray a worldview that looks like anthropocentrism, the environmental equivalent of sexism and racism, while lesser extremists will perhaps dislike her demonization of utilitarianism. If the previous evaluation of Marlow's study on nature language and imagery in Isaiah is correct, the following applications require further consideration: (1) Isaiah 1–39 reflects nature language and imagery as a consequence of the prophet living and ministering in an agrarian context, (2) since nature language and imagery is largely contextual, its presence reveals relatively little about the prophet's perceived view of humanity's relationship with the natural world (3) Isaiah's perception of non-human creation is anthropocentric and theocentric, with the natural world functioning as a reflection of man's sin and/or God's glory, (4) contemporary environmental ethicists cannot appeal to Isaiah 1–39 to defend the view that humanity and non-human creation hold equal inherent value, (5) since utilitarianism does not equal exploitation, Christians can affirm a biblical utilitarian anthropocentric view in relating to the natural world that proactively rejects exploitation and long-term damage, and (6) given the anthropocentric cause-and-effect relationship observed in the text, responsibility is to be placed upon humanity for the environmental status of the natural world, regardless of whether one is speaking about eating forbidden fruit or driving SUVs.

*Bibliography*

Borowski, O. *Agriculture in Iron Age Israel*. Winona Lake, IN: Eisenbrauns, 1987.

Childs, Brevard. *Isaiah*. Louisville, KY: Westminster John Knox, 2001.

Davis, Ellen F. *Scripture, Culture, and Agriculture: An Agrarian Reading of the Bible*. Cambridge: Cambridge University Press, 2008.

Marlow, Hilary. *Biblical Prophets and Contemporary Environmental Ethics: Rereading Amos, Hosea, and First Isaiah*. Oxford: Oxford University Press, 2009.

Wildberger, Hans. *Isaiah 1–12: A Commentary*. Translated by Thomas H. Trapp. Minneapolis, MN: Fortress, 1991.

## Is Breast Milk a "Kinship-Forging Substance" in the Hebrew Bible? A Response to Cynthia Chapman

Brian Peterson
Lee University, Cleveland, TN, USA

*Introduction*

This paper is a response to an article recently published in the *Journal for Hebrew Scriptures* by Cynthia R. Chapman. She proposes a thought-provoking argument, that breastfeeding (i.e., breast milk) in the ANE and ancient Israel (i.e., as evidenced in the Hebrew Bible) should be seen as paramount in forging kinship ties, even more so than blood relations.[1] Chapman utilizes a series of ANE and biblical texts to prove her proposed theory. While I have few issues with the concept, for Chapman has articulated more than a convincing argument from extra-biblical sources for such a position, I do think that her attempt to establish biblical precedence for her thesis is somewhat forced and unsustainable. For this reason, I will not focus on Chapman's use of ANE sources but will rather systematically assess the biblical evidence that she espouses as proof of the use of breast milk as a kinship-forging substance. Through this discussion I will conclude that Chapman's thesis needs to be reassessed and perhaps abandoned when it comes to the Hebrew Bible. The only text that appears to support her proposition is from the highly figurative Song of Songs. Even though her hypothesis *may* have been the reality for ancient Israelites, the texts cannot bear the weight of proof needed to sustain her argument.

---

1. Chapman, "Breast Milk," 1, argues that blood ties are more European in nature than Near Eastern.

## Isaiah 60:16; 49:23; 66:12–13

Chapman offers the "post-exilic" texts of Isa 60:16, 49:23, and 66:12–13 as support for her thesis. Beginning with Isa 60:16, she argues that the nations will suckle Jerusalem, thus, bestowing upon the holy city the "status-conferring properties of royal breast milk."[2] She translates v. 16 as follows, "You [Jerusalem] shall suck the milk of nations, you shall suck the breasts of kings, and you shall know that I, Yahweh, am your savior and your redeemer, the Mighty One of Jacob." She concludes this portion by noting that "When Zion sucks the milk of nations and sucks the breasts of kings, she acquires their traits and status, becoming royal and majestic herself."[3] There are two fundamental problems with this proposition. First, while Chapman acknowledges the metaphorical nature of the passage, it is clear that within the overall context of ch. 60, the author wants the reader to see that it is material wealth that is in view here, not royal status and traits *per se* (e.g., חיל "wealth" vv. 5, 11; זהב "gold" and לבונה "frankincense" v. 6; צאן "flocks" v. 7; כסף "silver" and זהב "gold" v. 9; foreigners will build Jerusalem's walls again v. 10; and the coveted lumber of Lebanon will come to Jerusalem v. 13). Now it is possible that one could argue that this material wealth will elevate Jerusalem to a "royal status" in a financial sense, for this would be a potential effect of any such transference of wealth. However, this is clearly tangible wealth, not abstract royal status, which appears to be Chapman's assertion here. Thus, from the overall context, the metaphor is clearly reflecting the idea of material support from the nations at the behest of God, not the transfer of "royal status" through metaphorical breast milk.[4]

---

2. Ibid., 12. Oswalt, *Book of Isaiah*, 552–53, suggests a similar reading although he goes on to stress the material support of Israel, not the royal nature of kings, *per se*.
3. Chapman, "Breast Milk," 12.
4. So too Watts, *Isaiah 34–66*, 296, and Leupold, *Exposition of Isaiah*, 314. Leupold points out the material aspect of the nations' support of Israel (i.e., the best of their "products").

Second, if breast milk is a "kinship-forging substance" as Chapman argues, it is very unlikely that Yahweh would want the newly constituted exilic community/Jerusalem to take on the "traits" of foreign nations, the very thing that had caused the exile in the first place (cf. Jeremiah 2; 44; Ezekiel 16; 23; 20:32; Hos 8:8; 9:1 etc.). What is more, it is Yahweh's glory/royal status that is being bestowed upon the people, not that of the nations.[5] Yahweh will not only make his people an "everlasting exaltation" (גאון עולם), he will also be in charge of bestowing their new status upon them (v. 17). Conversely, we see centripetal movement by nations and kings toward Israel, whom Yahweh has made the center of the nations (cf. Ezek 5:5; 38:12; Isa 2:2–3; Mic 4:1–2). For example, the nations are attracted to *Israel's* splendor (נגה), their kings are "drawn" (נהוגים Qal passive participle v. 11) to the *city*, nations' survivals are threatened if they do not serve (עבד) Israel (v. 12), and all who subjected them will bow (שחה) before them (v. 14). Thus, there is no foreign royal status being bestowed upon Israel; on the contrary, nations and kings are drawn to them.

In Isa 49:23 Chapman picks up on this same theme of the transfer of royalty through ingestion of breast milk. She renders the passage, "Kings will be your wet nurses, and their princesses will give you suck."[6] Again, in this metaphorical text, Chapman argues that "The result of this combined ingestion of royal breast milk is that the exiles will become like royals with those very same kings and princesses bowing down to them and licking the dust off their feet."[7] While aspects of points one and two in the above argument hold true here as well, a few further comments can be made. First, it is very impractical to assume that those

---

5. See for example the numerous references to Yahweh's glory and favor being transferred to the newly constituted city. E.g., Isa 60:1 כבוד יהוה עליך זרח (the glory of Yahweh has risen upon you); v. 2 וכבודו עליך יראה (and his [Yahweh's] glory will appear upon you); v. 9 כי פארך (for He [Yahweh] has glorified you); v. 10 וברצוני רחמתיך (and in my [Yahweh's] favor I have had compassion upon you); v. 19 ואלהיך לתפארתך (and your God as your glory).
6. Chapman, "Breast Milk," 12.
7. Ibid., 13.

who "lick the dust" off Israel's feet are of an elevated status over Israel, at least a status that merits transference of royalty through breastfeeding.[8] Second, the metaphor of v. 23 must be again read in the context of the chapter (esp. vv. 24–26), which suggests the exact opposite. Yahweh will in fact compel foreign royalty to deliver up the exiles and support them.[9] This seems to be the force of the metaphor, not transference of royalty. Third, as with Isaiah 60 it is Yahweh who gives the reconstituted nation its strength and glory, making them a light (אור) to the nations (cf. 49:6). Moreover, he causes princes to bow down before them (שחה v. 7) and makes Israel a "covenant" (ברית) for the nations (v. 8).[10] Interestingly, 49:15 even uses the metaphor of a woman with a nursing child (עול) but it is Yahweh who is being likened to the nursing woman (cf. v. 16), not the nations.[11]

Finally, in her dealing with Isa 66:12–13 Chapman is perhaps closest in keeping with her proposed thesis, especially by her inclusion of the discussion regarding the Judean pillar figurines from the 8th to 7th centuries BCE. Here, her argument takes on more force as Jerusalem metaphorically nurses the exiles.[12] She avers, "Here, one might imagine that the exiles return to their homeland carrying the foreign stain of Babylonia. Only through a rebirth by their capital city and through ingesting the milk of Jerusalem's breasts can they regain their ethnic status as the new Israelites marked by "glory," a repeated epithet of Yahweh's

---

8. So too Leupold, *Exposition of Isaiah*, 186–87. Blenkinsopp, *Isaiah 40–55*, 312–13, notes that the picture here of queens nursing Israel is a role befitting slaves, who often served as wet nurses (hardly an elevated status). He also points out that "licking the dust" of another's feet, in the context of royal settings would be "court protocol" for lesser kings/vassals before a king of much greater status. Again, this is hardly a desirable status to be conferred through breastfeeding. For a similar picture of licking the dust of one's feet in an ANE context, see the subservient act of Abimilki king of Tyre before Akhenaton where Abimilki likens himself to mere dirt, cf. "The Amarna Letters," translated by W. F. Albright (*ANET*, 484 esp. EA, No. 147).

9. So too Oswalt, *The Book of Isaiah*, 311.

10. See similar comments by Motyer, *Isaiah*, 395.

11. Verse 15 parallels a mother's attentiveness to her nursing child to Yahweh's attentiveness to Israel's needs.

12. Chapman, "Breast Milk," 14–17.

royal power."[13] In acknowledging the need for the exiles to regain their "ethnic status," Chapman undermines her argument in her first two proposed passages (i.e., Isa 60:16 and 49:23). In these earlier passages, she appears to be suggesting that Israel's consumption of the nations' breast milk only conferred royal status and not ethnic identity. This of course raises the question of how breast milk can be bifurcated in such a way even in a metaphorical sense. One is left wondering if this last passage may, in fact, be better explained as "nourishment and emotional bonding between God and Jerusalem," as Chapman points out in a footnote.[14]

One final note needs to be made regarding Chapman's inclusion of the Judean pillar figurines. Her survey of their use in Judean life and culture is persuasive. However, one must keep in mind the difference between that which is reflected in popular culture of the day (often interpreted from archaeological finds) and the theologically biased purview of the Hebrew Bible.[15] There can be no doubt that these figurines, along with other archaeological finds such as the Taanach Cult Stand and inscriptions like those found at Kuntillet Ajrud, point out a radically different perspective from that often portrayed in the Hebrew text.[16] As such, caution needs to be maintained when attempting

---

13. Ibid., 13.

14. Ibid., n. 58. So too the conclusions of Watts, *Isaiah 34–66*, 363, and Leupold, *Exposition of Isaiah*, 376.

15. This is often presented as the "Yahweh-alone" perspective. For a brief discussion on the development of monotheism in Israel, see Lang, *Monotheism and the Prophetic Minority*; Lang, "No God but Yahweh!"; Lang, "Zur Entstehung des biblischen Monotheismus."

16. For one interpretation of the 10th century BCE Taanach Stand, see J. Glen Taylor's works. He suggests that the first (i.e., the bottom level) and third levels of the stand depict Asherah and her image respectively, while levels two and four depict Yahweh (an absent deity between two cherubs) and his image (a horse and the sun disk between the two temple pillars) respectively. If this is the case, then the stand may reflect the popular religion of the day. See, Taylor, "Representations of Yahweh," 56–66; Taylor, *Yahweh and the Sun*, 24–37; Taylor, "Was Yahweh Worshipped as the Sun?" 55–59; Hess, *Israelite Religions*, 321–24. For notes on the Kuntillet Ajrud inscriptions, see Hess,

to prove certain facets of popular culture from the Hebrew Bible. This caution could also pertain to breast milk as a kinship-forging substance.

## Song of Songs 8:1–2

Next, Chapman's titular passage, Song of Songs 8:1–2, is indeed the most supportive of her thesis. Her exposition is compelling at key points, especially when she comments,

> The milk brother relationship described in 8:1 is an imagined relationship; the woman fantasizes that if her lover were her milk brother, several things would become possible. She [the female lover] insists that if he were a brother who had nursed at her mother's breasts, she could kiss him in public and no one would censure the activity. This suggests that public displays of physical affection between milk siblings were an accepted societal norm.[17]

Indeed, contextually, this is the intended meaning of the text. The young woman wants to have the freedom to express her affection to her lover/husband in public in the same way practiced by those who were next of kin (i.e., brother, father, or near relative, cf. Gen 29:11).[18] Where Chapman appears to falter is in her understanding of the phrase "mother's house," which she interprets in a literal sense. She notes, "The house of the mother, as a kinship designation and physical space specific to the mother, is precisely the location we would expect to find uterine and milk siblings residing together."[19] Here I must agree with Duane

---

*Israelite Religions*, 283–89; Smith, *Early History of God*, 118–25, esp. the bibliography on p. 118 n. 46.

17. Chapman, "Breast Milk," 18. So too the conclusion of Garrett, *Proverbs, Ecclesiastes, Song of Songs*, 424, and Pope, *Song of Songs*, 657.

18. Cf. Pope, *Song of Songs*, 657. ben Gershom, *Song of Songs*, 87, suggests that the reference to the brother who "sucked the breasts of my mother" is actually a nursing child not an adult *per se*. Hess, *Song of Songs*, 228 n. 59, notes an Egyptian love poem that presents a similar picture as v. 1 and the concerns about public displays of affection. Cf. also Keel, *Song of Songs*, 261, for comparisons with Egyptian love poetry where brother/sister terminology is used.

19. Chapman, "Breast Milk," 19.

Garrett's analysis that vv. 1 and 2 are not as closely tied grammatically as most English texts present them. He argues that v. 2 should read "I will lead you and bring you to *my mother's house*—she who has taught me. I would give you spiced wine to drink, the nectar of my pomegranates" (italics mine).[20] As Garrett correctly points out, "my mother's house" (בית אמי) here is a euphemism for the female reproductive parts.[21] This rendering would remove any suggestion of a tryst with a biological brother or lover in their mother's physical house where the woman and her brother had been conceived. The author is not referring to a literal place where "milk siblings reside together,"[22] but is expressing the female's desires in keeping with the highly symbolic language of the Song and the euphemistic overtones throughout. While I cannot be certain, it appears that Chapman is rejecting the idea that after ch. 4 of the Song, the two lovers are in fact experiencing conjugal relations as husband and wife.[23] Therefore the context of 8:1–2 is suggesting that even for a married woman, the simplest public displays of affection were inappropriate—something that saddens the newlywed. Therefore, because of this cultural taboo, the young woman instead will lead her beloved into an intimate moment of lovemaking, no doubt in the privacy of their *own* home.[24]

---

20. Garrett, *Proverbs, Ecclesiastes, and Song of Songs*, 423.

21. Garrett and House, *Song of Songs/Lamentations*, 172–73, 248–49. Hess, *Song of Songs*, 230, seems to hint at this as well by noting that "the instruction envisaged here is best understood as that of lovemaking and the joys of sexual pleasure . . ." On the other hand, Exum, *Song of Songs*, 247 (expressing basically the same position as Keel, *Song of Songs*, 261), points out the difficulty with the woman bringing her lover to her mother's house but misses the euphemism by suggesting that the lovers are so wrapped up in each other that they "give little thought to [social] convention"—a most unlikely ANE concept.

22. Chapman, "Breast Milk,"19.

23. Thus the conclusion of Fredericks and Estes, *Ecclesiastes and the Song of Songs*, 404–5, and Garrett and House, *Song of Songs/Lamentations*, 248.

24. So too Garrett, *Proverbs, Ecclesiastes, and Song of Songs*, 424 n. 180. However, contra Estes, who suggests that the couple are married and the woman is taking her lover to her mother's house: "the safest, most private place

In addition, one could just as easily argue that the wishful quip by the female lover in 8:1 referring to her beloved as a brother (i.e., "one who suckled at my mother's breasts") may simply be a stylized way of referring to her biological brother in a provocative manner. This definitely would be in keeping with the erotic tenor of the Song. The author may have no intention of promoting "breast milk as a kinship-forging substance" in which ethnic identity is being passed along as Chapman implies. On the contrary, the author may simply be continuing the highly figurative language, especially in light of v. 2. Now to be fair, this does not negate the possibility of Chapman's overall thesis. As a matter of fact, it is this passage that perhaps demonstrates her thesis most clearly—if that is indeed the intent of the original author. However, even though this may be the case, due to the highly figurative and euphemistic nature of the Song of Songs, and the tenuousness of the other texts she draws upon, her hypothesis cannot be sustained on this one text alone.

## *Hannah/Samuel and Manoah's Wife/Samson: 1 Samuel 1; Judges 13:3–5*

Chapman next moves into narrative literature, which one would expect to be less problematic when compared to the poetic and figurative language of Isaiah and the Song of Songs. This portion of her argument, on the surface, appears strong, especially in light of the Nazirite aspects that she teases out in these first two narratives. Chapman draws together the two stories of Hannah and Samuel and Samson and his mother. She states,

---

she knows." Cf. Fredericks and Estes, *Ecclesiastes and the Song of Songs*, 404. In ANE social conventions, the husband took the wife to his father's house not vice versa (cf. Genesis 24; 38; and Garrett and House, *Song of Songs/ Lamentations*, 172–73). Chapman, "Breast Milk," 19 n. 85, posits an interesting resolution to this problem by noting that the "house of the mother" is a sub-unit nested within the larger house of the father." However, based upon the highly symbolic language of the Song of Songs, the euphemistic interpretation fits best within the context.

The story of Samson's mother describes the prescribed maternal diet for a mother carrying a Nazirite; while the story of Hannah adds details concerning breastfeeding a Nazirite infant. Both stories provide evidence for the belief that a gestating and nursing mother had to adhere to the ritually prescribed diet of her Nazirite son.[25]

The strength of Chapman's argument for transference of ritual purity through a mother's breast milk is at first glance compelling. There can be no question in Judg 13:3–5 that there is a symbiotic relationship between the diet of the mother and the developing child and his status as a Nazirite. However, nowhere does the Judges' account mention breastfeeding.[26] Furthermore, the laws for the Nazirite in Num 6:1–5 make no such dietary prohibition on a pregnant woman. It is, perhaps, for this reason that an angel has to give Manoah's wife specific instructions in this regard—possibly a one-time prohibition (cf. Judg 13:4, 14)? On the other hand, Chapman's argument in the 1 Samuel passage rests heavily upon an argument from silence.[27] Nowhere is Hannah prescribed to keep a Nazirite diet like Manoah's wife.[28] It is clear that Chapman needed to bring the two accounts together in order to bolster her thesis.[29] One could just as easily argue from the pericope in 1 Samuel that the author was seeking to show the tender young age at which Samuel entered service in the tabernacle by the repeated use of the word for weaning (גמל, vv. 22, 23, 24). The Masoretic Text makes this fact clear in the use of נער ("youth"/"child") side by side in the phrase "now the

---

25. Chapman, "Breast Milk," 22.
26. It is only an assumption that the diet for Manoah's wife is directly tied to her breastfeeding, since the text is silent in this regard. One would expect that, if breastfeeding was of vital importance to Judges 13 as Chapman suggests, the text would be clearer than it is.
27. Chapman's argument could have been strengthened by referencing Cartledge, *1 and 2 Samuel*, 41, who brings out the importance of Hannah's breastfeeding of Samuel until he is weaned, as opposed to taking Samuel to Shiloh earlier and employing a wet nurse.
28. So too Miscall, *1 Samuel*, 13.
29. To be fair, Chapman is not the first to do this. There is precedence for these connections elsewhere. Cf. McCarter, *1 Samuel*, 65. Nevertheless, it is suspect in the context of what Chapman is trying to prove.

child *was very* young" (lit. "now the child was a child," והנער נער) in v. 24.³⁰ Moreover, as I will demonstrate in the Sarah/Isaac narrative, barren women who are granted the blessing of children tend to desire this privilege of breastfeeding, especially after the trauma of barrenness. Thus, Chapman's stance that breast milk plays a vital role in passing on ethnicity, at least in the 1 Samuel pericope, is tenuous at best.³¹

## Sarah and Isaac

Chapman's exposition of "three preposterous breastfeeding narratives" (Chapman's wording) includes Sarah's birthing and nursing of Isaac; Jochebed's nursing of Moses at the request of Pharaoh's daughter; and Naomi serving as a wet nurse for Obed. In all of these "tropes," Chapman avers that due to the presence of a foreigner/"outsider" (i.e., Hagar, Pharaoh's daughter, and Ruth respectively) the narrators needed to assure the reader that women of acceptable ethnic identity nursed these foundational males of Israel.

To begin with, Chapman contends that Sarah as a woman of status could have employed a wet nurse—the obvious choice being Hagar. However, because of the importance of breast milk to ethnic identity, Sarah opted to breastfeed Isaac herself as

---

30. So too, the rendering by the Tanakh and the NJB. Hertzberg, *I and II Samuel*, 28, suggests that based upon 2 Macc 7:27, Samuel was perhaps around three years old. Evans, *Message of Samuel*, 29, places Samuel's age possibly as old as five years. According to lactation consultants Jan Riordan and Karen Wambach, ancient societies generally stopped breastfeeding between 2–4 years of age based on a child's physiological needs and growth. See, Riordan and Wambach, *Breastfeeding and Human Lactation*, 52. For a discussion on the possible corruption of the MT here at v. 24, see Klein, *1 Samuel*, 3, and McCarter, *1 Samuel*, 56–57. S. R. Driver also points out the possibility that this is a textual error (see the similar reading of 4QSamᵃ) based on the LXX rendering as "the child was with them (והנער עמם)" but opts for "the child was *with her* (והנער עמה)." Cf. Driver, *Notes*, 21.

31. Chapman's inclusion of Pseudo-Philo is perhaps one of the most compelling pieces of information reinforcing her argument in the 1 Samuel story. However, because this is not a canonical text the strength of its witness is not overly helpful to her argument in the context of the canonical Hebrew Bible.

opposed to using a foreigner/"outsider." Again, several points can be made of graded significance. First, Chapman herself notes Rebekah's (Isaac's wife) similar elite status by pointing out that Rebekah had her own wet nurse (cf. Gen 24:59). This wet nurse is not only named (i.e., Deborah) but her death is also recorded (cf. Gen 35:8).[32] According to Chapman's reasoning, does this not allow for the possibility of Deborah (an "outsider") being a wet nurse to Jacob and Esau? In the case of Jacob, he is the very eponymous leader for the family/nation of Israel! Yet the text is silent about who exactly breastfed Jacob and Esau (cf. Gen 25:21–27). Second, Sarah's breastfeeding of Isaac must be understood in light of the preceding narratives (see esp. Genesis 16–18). That there was animosity between Hagar and Sarah because of Ishmael's birth is putting it mildly (cf. Gen 16:4, 6; 21:10). As such, one would well expect Sarah not to employ Hagar as a wet nurse for this very reason. Third, it had been 14 years since Hagar had borne Ishmael (cf. Gen 16:16 and 21:5). If she had weaned him at two to three years of age, the norm for the ANE, this would mean that she had not nursed a child for over 10 years. The text makes it clear that Hagar had only the one child (Gen 21:10–21). Therefore the odds of Hagar lactating after 10 years are low (see further discussions below for Naomi).[33]

Fourth, the biblical account of Isaac's nursing and weaning may be best explained on the grounds of Isaac's miraculous birth. Sarah had longed for a child so earnestly that she had insisted that her husband marry another woman (i.e., Hagar) in order to have a child. Thus, according to Gen 18:11–15 and 21:7, it is just as probable that Sarah nursed Isaac as part of the fulfillment of the miraculous event, and to bond with the child that she had always dreamed of having. I cannot imagine Sarah "farming out" this task, regardless of her status, after God had performed

---

32. Chapman, "Breast Milk," 28 n.133.
33. This is the same argument that can be made for Naomi. Modern lactation consultants do note the potential for a woman to start lactating after ceasing to breastfeed, but this takes weeks to accomplish, if it happens at all. Normally, this can occur within a few weeks or months of ceasing to breastfeed. Restarting after a period of years is uncommon.

such a miracle. In a similar vein, one could also ask the question as to why Sarah did not nurse Ishmael. If breast milk is a kinship-forging substance that can even be used to draw an "outsider's" child into ethnic unity with another's family, as suggested by Chapman in the Ruth-Naomi account, why would Sarah not force lactation and "adopt" Ishmael in this way?

Finally, according to anthropological studies, "in cultures that view breast milk as a conduit for ancestral power, it is not unusual for wet-nurses to be restricted to women of the mother's or father's clan and lineage."[34] This is the heart of Chapman's assertion about ancient Israel and the biblical accounts in question. According to this reality, Hagar would not have met the qualifications to begin with, thus removing the basis of Chapman's argument from the start. In all these debated texts, ancient readers would have automatically eliminated any foreign women (i.e., "outsiders") as unacceptable wet nurses.

Where I do think Chapman is correct is in her assessment of Sarah's timing of the "divorce" and expulsion of Hagar and Ishmael.[35] Some time after the weaning of Isaac and the ensuing celebrations would have been the opportune time, although we can only speculate on the elapsed time between Gen 21:8 and 9.

## *Moses and Jochebed*

Chapman's second "preposterous" breastfeeding text is that of Moses and Jochebed.[36] When Pharaoh's daughter found Moses floating in the bulrushes in a makeshift ark, Moses' sister (Miriam?) shows up and offers to procure wet-nursing services for the Egyptian's new-found son. Of course it is Moses' mother Jochebed who fills the role thus allowing *her* breast milk to transfer Levitical and Israelite ethnicity to Moses.

Chapman avers that the purpose of the opening portions of Exodus is to clarify the ethnic identity of Moses. She insists that

---

34. Riordan and Wambach, *Breastfeeding and Human Lactation*, 807. For the actual study see van Esterik and Elliott, "Infant Feeding Style," 183–95.
35. Chapman, "Breast Milk," 30.
36. Ibid., 30–33.

the author informs the reader through this breastfeeding account that Moses is in fact Israelite, a Levite at that. The biggest downside of Chapman's assertion is that she does not explain to the reader why Pharaoh's daughter would not have insisted on an Egyptian wet nurse if in fact the important connection between breast milk and ethnic identity was so well known in the ANE—a reality her paper presents very persuasively throughout. While it is possible that the text is a "literary trope of mocking the Egyptians"[37] one still must answer the question as to why Pharaoh's daughter would have overlooked this "elephant in the room." Moreover, is it not just as possible that the breastfeeding account is included to show God's compassionate intervention in the midst of the human carnage implied in Exodus 1? The reader is brought into the heart-wrenching story of Exodus 2 by witnessing and feeling the emotional pain of Jochebed as she attempts to hide and keep her beautiful (טוב) boy from certain death for three months (Exod 2:2). The resolution to the conflict in the text comes when Moses is given back to Jochebed so she can raise the child in the open and with Pharaoh's financial support (Exod 2:9). If Pharaoh's daughter did know about the importance of breast milk ethnicity connections, the text makes it clear that she cannot overpower the plans and purposes of Yahweh, a similar situation evinced in the hardening of Pharaoh's heart.[38] The irony of the text is fitting, but more importantly it shows the protection of God's chosen leader from birth (note also a similar theme in Joseph's life immediately before in Genesis 39–50).[39] The text thus depicts how Jochebed was afforded the opportunity to raise and coddle her child in the midst of infanticidal chaos by means of the most intimate act available to a mother, breastfeeding.

37. Ibid., 31. She notes Propp's assertion of this fact. Cf. Propp, *Exodus 1–18*, 154.
38. There are 14 references to the hardening of Pharaoh's heart (Exod 7:13, 22; 8:15, 19, 32; 9:7, 12, 34, 35; 10:1, 20, 27; 11:10; 14:8). In no less than six of these cases, the Lord does the hardening of the god-like Pharaoh (Exod 9:12; 10:1, 20, 27; 11:10; 14:8).
39. Note similar protective motifs in "The Birth Legend of Sargon of Akkad," translated by Benjamin R. Foster (*COS* 1.133:461).

Finally, Chapman does not address the fact that Jochebed had already nursed Moses for a period of three months (cf. Exod 2:2). This is not only implied in the text, it is made explicit when Moses' sister quickly *finds* someone to "nurse" Moses for his new royal mother (Exod 2:7–9).[40] In light of this, one must answer the question as to how long a child has to be breastfed before he/she is ethnically linked to the desired family. If Naomi's possible "symbolic" breastfeeding of Obed is sufficient (Chapman's suggestion—see next section below), is Jochebed's nursing of Moses for three months sufficient? Again, Chapman passes over this issue.

## Naomi and Obed

Chapman's final "preposterous" breastfeeding narrative is, perhaps, the least convincing textual example she puts forward in her article. Her assertion that Naomi became a wet nurse to Obed in order to pass on her ethnic identity to her grandson due to Ruth's tainted Moabite pedigree is strained on several levels.

First, Chapman's premise that, because Ruth is a foreigner (נכרי Ruth 2:10), she cannot pass on acceptable ethnicity to Obed, even though she has sworn loyalty oaths to Naomi, her people, and her God, is not convincing (Ruth 1:16–17). Throughout Israel's history, men of war were known to have captured foreign women who later became their wives (cf. Num 31:18). The book of Deuteronomy presents legislation that is meant to elucidate and give instruction on this very practice (Deut 21:10–14). In these cases, ethnicity was not a matter of concern for Yahweh or the people.[41] Second, and along the same lines of

---

40. The Hebrew word ינק ("to nurse") is used twice in v. 7 as both a participle and a verb and twice in v. 9. This is the term normally used for wet nurses and nursing in general (e.g., Gen 21:7; 24:59; 32:16; Num 11:12; Deut 32:25; 1 Sam 1:23 etc.).

41. I am aware that Chapman narrows her arguments to men of status (i.e., Isaac, Moses, and Obed/David) but this neither answers the question as to why Isaac, and not Jacob is given a breastfeeding narrative, nor does it solve the problem of why David's own mother is not brought into the narratives in a breastfeeding incident. On p. 40, Chapman suggests that there was no foreign

argument, are the genealogical lists of the New Testament. The entry on Obed, David's grandfather, in the New Testament Gospel of Matthew, whose audience was clearly Jewish, lists not only Ruth (1:5), but Tamar (1:3) and Rahab (1:5), in the lineage of Jesus. Obviously as of the first century CE ethnic connections to these foreign women were not an issue either. Surprisingly, Naomi is never mentioned again in the Bible after Ruth 4:17, whereas Ruth is.

Third, Chapman goes against almost all commentators and several modern translations in her assertion that Naomi was, in fact, a literal wet nurse to Obed based upon the language of Ruth 4:16.[42] Chapman translates v. 16 as follows, "Naomi took the child and placed him at her *breast*, and she became his *wet nurse*" (italics mine).[43] Chapman focuses on the Hebrew word אמנת (Qal participle feminine) insisting that it can have the connotation of "wet nurse" even though it has a wide semantic range being used of both males and females and with the nuance of both a wet nurse and a guardian (e.g., Num 11:12; Esth 2:20; 2 Kgs 10:1; Isa 49:23).[44] What is more, the inclusion of the word

---

or slave woman in the narrative of Rebekah; thus, solving the problem for why there was no breastfeeding narrative for Jacob. However, earlier in her article (cf. p. 28 n. 133), she points out that Rebekah had her own wet nurse (however old she was, cf. Gen 24:59 and 35:8).

42. So Bush, *Ruth/Esther*, 259; Sasson, *Ruth*, 172; Campbell, *Ruth*, 164; Younger, *Judges/Ruth*, 483; Block, *Judges, Ruth*, 730. For a discussion on the possibility of Naomi's actions serving as a legal adoption, see Köhler, "Die Adoptionsform," 312–14. For a refutation of Köhler, see Joüon, *Ruth*, 94, or Campbell, *Ruth*, 165. Two proponents of the "wet nurse" interpretation are de Waard and Nida, *Book of Ruth*, 79, as cited by Bush, *Ruth/Esther*, 259. For modern translations that go against Chapman's reading, cf. NIV, NLT, and TNK. Most other translations use the generic term "nurse" with no connotations of "wet nursing," cf. NAS, NRS, NKJ, ESV, etc.

43. Chapman, "Breast Milk," 35.

44. Chapman spends three pages (pp. 36–38) giving examples where the root אמן *may* be understood in the technical sense of "wet nurse." However, several of these must be understood in the figurative sense. Furthermore, Bush, *Ruth/Esther*, 258–59, duly notes that the "feminine form [of אמנת] occurs in one passage (other than Ruth 4:16) to refer to the "nurse" of the *five-year-old* Mephibosheth (cf. 2 Sam 4:4). Hence, it is quite clear that the word is used to mean "nurse" in the sense of the one who takes care of or looks after a child."

חיק ("lap"), which never means "breast," helps clarify that wet nursing is not in play.⁴⁵ Even though Chapman correctly points out that the normal Hebrew term for wet nurse is מינקת from the root ינק ("to nurse" cf. Gen 24:59; 35:8; Exod 2:7; 2 Kgs 11:2; 2 Chron 22:11), she does not answer the question as to why the author did not use the less ambiguous term.⁴⁶ If breast milk as a kinship-forging substance was so important and central to the account, why would the author not use one of these clearer terms as opposed to the more cryptic term אמנת?⁴⁷

Fourth, while there is some evidence of "grandmothers" in African and other cultural contexts nursing their grandchildren (i.e., premenopausally),⁴⁸ the very idea that a "post-menopausal"

Bush rightly notes that the chances of Mephibosheth still being nursed at five years of age are slim.

45. So Bush, *Ruth/Esther*, 257, and Block, *Judges/Ruth*, 730 (as does Campbell, *Ruth*, 164–65), correctly point out that the combination of חיק ("the front of one's body" cf. 2 Sam 12:3) and אמנת ("guardian" or "nanny"), terms used of both men and women, should not be forced into being read as "wet nurse" in the context.

46. Chapman, "Breast Milk," 36 n. 171.

47. So too Sasson, *Ruth*, 172.

48. Slome, "Nonpuerperal Lactation in Grandmothers," 550–52. Slome lists five cases of Zulu women who ranged in age from 45 to 48 who suckled their grandchildren. In most cases these women had had several of their own children and all but one was still *premenopausal*. In the one case where the grandmother was postmenopausal, lactation did not occur. The elapsed time from the weaning of their own children until the suckling of their grandchild ranged from 2 to 15 years, most falling into the lower range. Slome cites two other studies of African tribes that do appear to attest to post-menopausal grandmothers lactating. These studies are: Bryant, *The Zulu People,* 631, and Barlow and Buchan, "Non-Puerperal Lactation," 976. However, in the former study, no scientific or medical analysis was done; it was merely general observations by the author, a historian (cf. Bryant's own comments in his preface concerning the unscientific nature of his research of the Zulu tribe, pp. xi–xiv). In the latter case, one woman was observed at age 55 who breastfed her grandchild eight years after her own child had been weaned. No mention is made of her menopausal state in this brief notation. Cf. also David Livingston, *Missionary Travels,* 140. Livingston records one event where a grandmother had nursed her grandchild. He goes on to note that the grandmother "at least forty years of age" (no doubt again premenopausal). Finally, H. A. Wieschhoff, "Artificial Stimulation," 1403–15, compiled a wealth of examples from around

(Chapman's wording) woman would become a wet nurse is problematic especially after not having children for at least 20 years.[49] According to breastfeeding and lactation specialists Jan Riordan and Karen Wambach, lactation in women involves a two-stage process: endocrine and autocrine. The endocrine stage is hormonal, brought on by a woman's pregnancy, whereby she produces colostrum (i.e., nutrient-rich milk full of proteins and immunoglobulins produced at the end of pregnancy). The autocrine stage begins when a baby starts to nurse.[50] Thus, pregnancy is what triggers lactation, and Naomi was not currently pregnant. While it is possible for a "woman to stimulate lactation without a recent pregnancy," it is rare.[51] Riordan and Wambach go on to tell the story of a 40-year-old woman who adopted a child and decided to breastfeed. They note the many "challenges of inducing lactation beginning one month before the birth using breast stimulation via pumping and use of

---

the world in relation to grandmothers suckling grandchildren. In every case presented where the grandmothers were premenopausal (i.e., 30 to late 40s in age), lactation at some level occurred. For women at or near menopause (around 50 years of age) the lactation that did occur was insufficient to sustain the child and in one case actually caused the infant to die of apparent malnutrition. In all these cases, the older the woman was the longer it took to begin lactation (3 to 10 or more days). Wieschhoff (1414) notes only one documented case in France of a woman 71 years of age suckling a child after a 25 year lapse in breastfeeding. He notes that this is an obvious "abnormality." He concludes, "It should be emphasized . . . that in no instance has a careful physical examination been made by those who report its [lactation] occurrence, so that we are dealing with impressionistic accounts. . . . what may be termed cultural fiction" (1414–15).

49. Chapman, "Breast Milk," 36. Mahlon and Chilion were obviously of adult age and were married. A conservative estimate from the time Naomi had her last child until he died must have been at least 20 years, if not more (i.e., see the notation of the family living in Moab for 10 years in 1:4). So too, Bush, *Ruth/Esther*, 259, and Sasson, *Ruth*, 172, who note the improbability of Naomi serving as a wet nurse at such an advanced age. Note that Bush, *Ruth/Esther*, 259, goes on to reject Sasson's (235–37) suggestion of a parallel between ANE goddesses suckling infants and Ruth 4:16 on the basis that there is no "vestigial motif" here in the text.

50. Riordan and Wambach, *Breastfeeding and Human Lactation*, 92.

51. Ibid., 52.

domperidone and oxytocin spray. A lactation consultant, a midwife, and a birth mother, who was a relative, supported this mother during the rigorous process."[52] In this rare case, the use of modern drugs and pumps was necessary, both of which were not at Naomi's disposal.[53] Lactation specialist Christine Sneed adds that, while it is true that women can force lactation without ever having a child, this is generally only possible in women *before* menopause—even then the woman rarely if ever can produce enough milk to meet the demand of a child.[54] Given these assertions of lactation experts, it is virtually impossible to believe Chapman's assertion that a postmenopausal Naomi breastfed Obed. It appears that Chapman recognizes the tenuousness of her suggestion that Naomi became a literal wet nurse because she posits the possible "symbolic" nature of the action

---

52. Ibid., 827. Cheales-Siebenaler, "Induced Lactation," 42–43, relates an account where an adoptive mother induced lactation but still required modern drugs and pumps. She concluded that no "measurable amount of milk was pumped until the baby was four months old." For traditional methods of inducing lactation, see Mead, *Sex and Temperament*, or Lawrence, *Breastfeeding*, esp. ch. 17. These methods include herbal teas and coconut milk (as cited by Biervliet et al., "Induction of Lactation," 582). On the use of herbs and galactogogues in traditional cultures, see Riordan and Wambach, *Breastfeeding and Human Lactation*, 810. Note, however, that in the cases where traditional medicines and herbs are used, women are generally already nursing and are seeking to increase milk production. Riordan and Wambach, *Breastfeeding and Human Lactation*, 531–32, suggest this has more of a placebo effect that anything else. See also Wieschhoff, "Artificial Stimulation," 1406–9 for a discussion on traditional African lactating remedies. Wieschhoff is also dubious of these traditional "remedies" for lactation (1414).

53. For a chart of this detailed regimen, see Riordan and Wambach, *Breastfeeding and Human Lactation*, 532.

54. Christine Sneed, personal communication. Cf. also Bryant, "Nursing the Adopted Infant," 374–79, esp. 378, where she notes that rarely will this method produce enough milk to sustain a child. See a similar conclusion in the case study by Biervliet et al., "Induction of Lactation," 581–83. Medical practitioners Kinga A. Szucs, Sherry Axline, and Marc Rosenman do report a case whereby an adoptive premenopausal mother produced enough breast milk through induced lactation to meet the needs of twins. See their article, "Induced Lactation," 309–13. For a further bibliography on the topic, see Dennis, "Breastfeeding Initiation and Duration."

as well.⁵⁵ However, she draws upon symbolic wet-nurse examples from much later Islamic and Irish settings. The time span between the story of Ruth and these later texts is a problem, not to mention the cultural differences of the latter case. Furthermore, how is "symbolic" nursing supposed to pass on ethnic identity if this suggested status resides in the breast milk?⁵⁶

Finally, Chapman suggests that the author of Ruth stresses Ruth's Moabite/foreign identity (a negative—thus the reason Naomi had to breastfeed Obed) by using the phrase "Ruth the Moabite" throughout. She avers that this is the case until Ruth marries Boaz, at which time the heroine becomes simply "Ruth" and is quickly replaced in the narrative by Naomi (4:13).⁵⁷ However, the text is somewhat divided in its use of both references. The appellation "Ruth" is used seven times (cf. 1:4, 14, 16; 2:8, 22; 3:9; 4:13) in four chapters whereas the phrase "Ruth the Moabitess" is used only five times (cf. 1:22; 2:2, 21; 4:5, 10). Therefore the usage may be stylistic as opposed to a means of negatively emphasizing Ruth's ethnicity in some way. In light of the numerous problems with this textual example, Chapman's proposal again appears somewhat dubious.⁵⁸

---

55. Chapman, "Breast Milk," 38.

56. While the "symbolic" concept could be argued for the metaphors of Isaiah, which Chapman musters as evidence (see above), here in these three "preposterous breastfeeding accounts" the text wants to be read in a literal sense.

57. Chapman, "Breast Milk," 38–39. Chapman points out that Ruth is never mentioned by name after v. 13, thus heightening the role of Naomi as breast-milk provider. However, Ruth is addressed indirectly, and with glowing praise, in v. 15. Technically, there are only two more narrative verses after v. 15 before the genealogical list. It is very odd to assume that Ruth has been lowered or removed from the picture because of her foreignness when, in essence, she receives the highest praise from all of the ladies of the region.

58. Based upon the historical setting (cf. Ruth 1:1) it is possible that the use of the phrase "Ruth the Moabitess" may have been added by a later editor. This may have been done to contrast the upright nature of Ruth, a foreigner, who is keeping the Law of Yahweh as opposed to the Canaanization of the Israelites in the book of Judges.

## Some Final Notes

Chapman makes several arguments from silence. She states,

> We also do not have breast milk source identification when that identification would hurt or work against the desired ethnic presentation of the foundational male. Tamar, the Canaanite, is not described as nursing Perez. Joseph's Egyptian wife is not shown to nurse Ephraim. Bathsheba does not nurse Solomon. In each of these households, there is no insider woman who could be brought into service as Naomi was for Obed.[59]

While most of these observations are indeed true, it does not warrant a blanket statement suggesting that breastfeeding narratives are absent because these women are/may be "outsiders." One glaring problem is with her questioning of Bathsheba's tribal identity.[60] A close reading of the text suggests that Bathsheba is from the tribe of Judah. Yes, Bathsheba was the daughter of Eliam (2 Sam 11:3) as Chapman notes, but 2 Sam 23:34 goes on to identify Eliam as the son of Ahithophel the Gilonite, from the region of Judah.[61] This is the most acceptable tribe for a king to be from! Solomon had a double ethnic connection to his home tribe through both his mother and father.

Finally, in a footnote, Chapman suggests that the Deuteronomist "provides the subtle clue" that Joash's breastfeeding was outsourced to a wet nurse to shield him from the "stain" of Athaliah's ethnicity (i.e., the house of Ahab cf. 2 Kgs 11:1–3;

---

59. Chapman, "Breast Milk," 40.
60. Ibid., 40 n. 185.
61. The inclusion of Eliam along with Uriah the Hittite's name in the identification of Bathsheba seems to indicate some importance for her father (so McCarter, *II Samuel*, 285, 499, and Anderson, *2 Samuel*, 153). Even though some may question the significance, I agree with both Herzberg and Mauchline in their positive identity of Ahithophel as Bathsheba's grandfather, especially when one considers the actions of Ahithophel in siding with David's conspirators during the revolt of Absalom (cf. 2 Sam 15–17). He must have had a good reason for doing so, viz., to get revenge for David's actions against Uriah and his granddaughter. Cf. Hertzberg, *I and II Samuel*, 309–10; Mauchline, *I and 2 Samuel*, 248–49. See also comments by Schley, "Ahithophel," 121–22, and Jewish interpreters in *Sanhedrin* 69b, 101a. On the location of Giloh in Judah, cf. Mazar, "Giloh," 1027–28, and McCarter, *II Samuel*, 357.

2 Chron 22:10–12).[62] However, Joash's mother is clearly listed as Zibiah of Beersheba (2 Kgs 12:1; 2 Chron 24:1) with no apparent relation to Athaliah. Why would the Deuteronomist seek to mention an unnamed wet nurse of perhaps questionable ethnicity when Joash's ethnicity could have been bolstered by Zibiah's clearly stated Judahite connections? Therefore there was no need for a wet nurse's breast milk to cleanse the "stain" of Athaliah's lineage when Joash's biological mother could have served the purpose more effectively.

## Conclusion

As I have demonstrated throughout, in most cases Chapman's thesis raises more questions than it answers. There can be little doubt that both relatively modern and ANE cultures (perhaps even Israel's) placed importance upon breast milk as a kinship-forging substance, something Chapman does an excellent job of demonstrating. However, when it comes to the biblical examples, her evidence is tenuous at best. It is clear that in every biblical case marshaled by Chapman (perhaps with the exception of Song of Songs 8:1–2), either alternate explanations can be offered for the presence of breastfeeding narratives or her thesis falters on grammatical, medical, and/or logical grounds. Until some of these concerns are addressed, if they can be at all, I remain unconvinced by Chapman's proposal.

## Bibliography

Anderson, A. A. *2 Samuel*. WBC 11. Dallas: Word, 1989.

Barlow Margaret, and B. M. A. Buchan. "Non-Puerperal Lactation." *South African Medical Journal* 29 no. 4 (1955) 976.

---

62. Chapman, "Breast Milk," 40 n. 186. She notes that Joash is the only king from Judah who has a wet nurse mentioned in the text.

ben Gershom, Levi. *Commentary on Song of Songs*. Translated by Menachem Kellner. New Haven: Yale University Press, 1998.

Biervliet, F. P., et al. "Induction of Lactation in the Intended Mother of a Surrogate Pregnancy: Case Report." *Human Reproduction* 16 (2000) 581–83.

Blenkinsopp, Joseph. *Isaiah 40–55*. AB 19A. New York: Doubleday, 2000.

Block, Daniel. *Judges, Ruth*. NAC 6. Nashville: Broadman & Holman, 1999.

Bryant, Alfred T. *The Zulu People: As They Were before the White Man Came*. Pietermaritzburg: Shuter & Shooter, 1949; repr., New York: Negro Universities Press, 1970.

Bryant, Cathy A. "Nursing the Adopted Infant." *Journal of the American Board of Family Medicine* 19 (2006) 374–79.

Bush, Frederic. *Ruth/Esther*. WBC 9. Waco, TX: Word, 1996.

Campbell, Edward F. *Ruth*. AB 7. Garden City, NY: Doubleday, 1975.

Cartledge, Tony W. *1 and 2 Samuel*. Macon, GA: Smyth & Helwys, 2001.

Chapman, Cynthia R. "'Oh that you were like a brother to me, one who had nursed at my mother's breasts': Breast Milk as a Kinship-Forging Substance." *Journal of Hebrew Scriptures* 12 (2012) 1–41.

Cheales-Siebenaler, Noreen J. "Induced Lactation in an Adoptive Mother." *Journal of Human Lactation* 15 (1999) 41–43.

de Waard J., and E. A. Nida. *A Translator's Handbook on the Book of Ruth*. London: United Bible Societies, 1973.

Dennis, C. "Breastfeeding Initiation and Duration: A 1999–2000 Literature Review." *Journal of Obstetric Gynecologic and Neonatal Nursing* 31 (2001) 12–32.

Driver, S. R. *Notes on the Hebrew Text of Samuel*. London: Oxford University Press, 1889; repr., Winona Lake, IN: Alpha, 1984.

Evans, Mary J. *The Message of Samuel*. Downers Grove, IL: InterVarsity, 2004.

Exum, J. Cheryl. *Song of Songs*. Louisville: Westminster John Knox, 2005.

Fredericks, Daniel, and Daniel Estes. *Ecclesiastes and the Song of Songs*. AOTC 16. Downers Grove, IL: InterVarsity, 2010.

Garrett, Duane. *Proverbs, Ecclesiastes, Song of Songs*. NAC 14. Nashville: Broadman, 1993.

Garrett, Duane, and Paul House. *Song of Songs/Lamentations*. WBC 23B. Nashville: Thomas Nelson, 2004.

Hertzberg, Hans Wilhelm. *I and II Samuel*. Translated by J. S. Bowden. Philadelphia: Westminster, 1976.

Hess, Richard. *Israelite Religions: An Archaeological and Biblical Survey*. Grand Rapids: Baker Academic, 2007.

———. *Song of Songs*. Grand Rapids: Baker Academic, 2005.

Joüon, Paul. *Ruth: Commentaire Philologique et Exégétique*. Rome: Institut Biblique Pontifical, 1924, repr. 1953.

Keel, Othmar. *The Song of Songs*. Translated by Frederick J. Glaiser. Minneapolis: Fortress, 1994.

Klein, Ralph W. *1 Samuel*. WBC 10. Waco TX: Word, 1983.

Köhler, L. "Die Adoptionsform von Ruth 4,16." *ZAW* 29 (1909) 312–14.

Lang, Bernhard. *Monotheism and the Prophetic Minority: An Essay in Biblical History and Sociology*. The Social World of Biblical Antiquity. Sheffield: Almond, 1983.

———. "No God but Yahweh! The Origin and Character of Biblical Monotheism." *Con* 177 (1985) 41–49.

———. "Zur Entstehung des biblischen Monotheismus." *TQ* 166 (1986) 135–42.

Lawrence, R. A. *Breastfeeding: A Guide for the Medical Profession*. 4th ed. St. Louis: Mosby Year Book, 1994.

Leupold, Herbert C. *Exposition of Isaiah: Volume II Chapters 40–66*. Grand Rapids: Baker, 1971.

Livingston, David. *Missionary Travels and Researches in South Africa*. New York: Harper, 1858.

Mauchline, John. *1 and 2 Samuel*. London: Oliphants, 1971.

Mazar, Amihay. "Giloh." *ABD* 2:1027–28.

McCarter, P. Kyle, Jr. *I Samuel*. AB 8. Garden City, NY: Doubleday, 1980.

———. *II Samuel*. AB 9. Garden City, NY: Doubleday, 1984.

Mead, M. *Sex and Temperament in Three Primitive Societies*. New York: Dell, 1963.

Miscall, Peter D. *1 Samuel: A Literary Reading*. Bloomington: Indiana University Press, 1986.

Motyer, J. Alec. *The Prophecy of Isaiah: An Introduction and a Commentary*. Downers Grove, IL: InterVarsity, 1993.

Oswalt, John. *The Book of Isaiah: Chapters 40–66*. Grand Rapids: Eerdmans, 1998.

Pope, Marvin. *Song of Songs*. AB 7C. Garden City: Doubleday, 1977.

Propp, William. *Exodus 1–18: A New Translation with Introduction and Commentary*. AB 2. New York: Doubleday, 1999.

Riordan, Jan, and Karen Wambach. *Breastfeeding and Human Lactation*. 4th ed. Sudbury, MA: Jones & Bartlett, 2010.

Sasson, Jack. *Ruth: A New Translation with a Philological Commentary and a Formalist-Folklorist Interpretation*. Baltimore: Johns Hopkins University Press, 1979.

Schley, D. G. "Ahithophel." *ABD* 1:121–22.

Slome, Cecil. "Nonpuerperal Lactation in Grandmothers." *Journal of Paediatrics* 49 (1956) 550–52.

Smith, Mark. *The Early History of God*. 2nd ed. Grand Rapids: Eerdmans, 2002.

Szucs, Kinga A., Sherry Axline, and Marc Rosenman. "Induced Lactation and Exclusive Breast Milk Feeding of Adopted Premature Twins." *Journal of Human Lactation* 26 (2010) 309–13.

Taylor, J. Glen. "The Two Earliest Known Representations of Yahweh." In *Ascribe to the Lord: Biblical and Other Studies in Memory of Peter C. Craigie*, edited by L. Eslinger and G. Taylor, 56–66. JSOTSup 67. Sheffield: JSOT Press, 1988.

———. "Was Yahweh Worshipped as the Sun?" *BAR* 20.3 (1994) 55–59.

———. *Yahweh and the Sun: Biblical and Archaeological Evidence for Sun Worship in Ancient Israel*. JSOTSup 111. Sheffield: JSOT, 1993.

van Esterik, P., and T. Elliott. "Infant Feeding Style in Urban Kenya." *Ecology of Food and Nutrition* 18 no. 3 (1986) 183–95.

Watts, John D. W. *Isaiah 34–66*. WBC 25. Waco, TX: Word, 1987.

Wieschhoff, H. A. "Artificial Stimulation of Lactation in Primitive Cultures." *Bulletin of the History of Medicine* 8.10 (1940) 1403–15.

Younger, K. Lawson, Jr. *Judges/Ruth*. Grand Rapids: Zondervan, 2002.

## Has the True Meaning and Purpose of the Lord's Prayer Been Lost? A Sociolinguistic Study of the Lord's Prayer in Dialogue with Wilson-Kastner and Crossan

Hughson T. Ong
McMaster Divinity College, Hamilton, ON, Canada

### Introduction

My objective in this article is to show that Jesus' immediate concern in teaching his own prayer to his disciples was to teach them that it was important for them to pray, and that they must pray with the right motive and attitude. I agree that the content of the prayer serves as a model, but I do not believe that this is the focus of the passages where it appears.

Since the time Jesus taught it, the Lord's Prayer has not only become a significant part of the believer's life and the liturgy of the church,[1] but it has also received much scholarly attention.[2] In our postmodern context today, where there seems to be a great need for both human transformation and the transformation of

---

1. The Lord's Prayer has established a special place in church liturgy and personal prayers. Palmer, *The Lord's Prayer*, 8, refers to it as the "love-song of the Christian world"; Marty, *Hidden Discipline*, 83, calls it "a battle cry, a shout for the end time."

2. The bibliography for the Lord's Prayer is large, but an excellent classic resource is Jeremias, *Prayers of Jesus*. Apart from the various renditions into different languages and biblical and liturgical versions of the Lord's Prayer (see Porter, "Translations of the Bible," 366–68, for E. Nida's excellent study on the liturgical structure and translation of the Lord's Prayer), the Lord's Prayer has also been interpreted through John 17, the Pauline epistles, and 1 Peter. See Ayo, *The Lord's Prayer*, 225–44. Many have pointed out the connection, as well as the distinction between the prayer that Jesus taught (the Lord's Prayer) and the prayer that he himself prayed (John 17). See Chase, *The Lord's Prayer*, 110–11; Walker, "The Lord's Prayer"; Brooke, "The Lord's Prayer."

the world system, the Lord's Prayer continues to receive such unabated attention because of its practical value for Christian living. Of course, there is nothing wrong with this, but I strongly believe that the true meaning and original purpose of the Lord's Prayer are often overlooked when practicality and application become the central focus, that is, when we ignore its original historical and sociolinguistic contexts in our interpretation.

Two scholarly works that exemplify such practical goals for the study of the Lord's Prayer are Patricia Wilson-Kastner's "Pastoral Theology and the Lord's Prayer" and John Dominic Crossan's *The Greatest Prayer*.[3] As a practical theologian, Wilson-Kastner offers her theological reflection on the Lord's Prayer and raises two issues concerning the correlation between preaching and the Lord's Prayer, as well as the pastoral and theological implications of the prayer.[4] With reference to preaching, she asks whether the pattern of the prayer is appropriate for sermons by virtue of the prayer's prominent status in the Sunday worship service, Morning Prayer, and the celebration of the Eucharist. Accordingly, she points out that the Lord's Prayer raises all kinds of pastoral and theological issues for the preacher and subsequently mentions nine interrelated issues in which the Lord's Prayer becomes relevant to contemporary human reality.[5]

---

3. There are, of course, many other works in this regard. However, my decision to mention these two is largely because of my own concern, as a New Testament scholar, for both the exegetical and practical aspects of New Testament studies. Whereas Crossan's position may be seen as a more liberal construal of the Lord's Prayer that can be contrasted with my more conservative sociolinguistic interpretation of the prayer from within the New Testament's horizon, Wilson-Kastner's position represents an interpretation of the Lord's Prayer from the pastoral and theological end.

4. Although Wilson-Kastner had a PhD in World Religions, she fully recognized her calling as a practicing minister of the church. In an interview by the Greensboro *Daily News* in August 1974 she said, "My ideal of what a theologian ought to be was what you have in the early church, a practicing minister who writes about and reflects upon the faith of the Christian. I didn't want to be a minister or just be a professor" (cited in Reyman, "Finding Aid for Patricia Wilson-Kastner Papers, 1944–1998," 2–3).

5. See Wilson-Kastner, "Pastoral Theology."

Crossan's proposal, on the other hand, can in various ways be seen as a novel (and postmodern) way of construing God's kingdom as the new egalitarian community Jesus inaugurated during his earthly life, in which Christians are called to collaborate through the Lord's Prayer. He lists five themes that he claims are interwoven, and contends that they emerged out of the first-century Roman socio-political context, where the early believers prayed the Lord's Prayer under an imperial government that had a different world system.[6] Despite living under such an awful world government, Christians were called to pray in collaboration with God's universal plan of equity and justice for the world—the God of the Lord's Prayer is a God of nonviolent distributive justice and not a God of violent retributive justice.[7] Thus, Crossan asks, if God is a nonviolent God, is the person who taught this prayer a representative of violence or non-violence?[8] This is what he seeks to explain by exploring the biblical tradition of each phrase of the prayer through the lens of biblical Hebrew poetry.[9]

While these values and purposes of the Lord's Prayer are important (and I agree with much that these scholars say), I

---

6. These five themes are: (1) the translation of πατήρ by the more appropriate term "householder" rather than "father"; (2) human beings as co-householders or stewards of the divine householder; (3) Jesus as the Heir (not the Son, a patriarchal term) of God; (4) Christians as co-collaborators with Christ; and (5) how all the above themes converge in the Lord's Prayer to show that it is "both a revolutionary manifesto and a hymn of hope . . . from the heart of Judaism through the mouth of Christianity to the conscience of the earth" (Crossan, *The Greatest Prayer*, 181–82).

7. Crossan, *The Greatest Prayer*, 2–3, points out that true "justice" is not retributive but distributive, which means an equitable distribution of everything.

8. Crossan challenges us "to think about Jesus as the creator of the *Abba* Prayer and to ask ourselves: Do we find any violence in it? Or do we find in it—and in the life that produces it as its summary—a nonviolent vision that is still the last best hope for our species and our earth?" (Crossan, *The Greatest Prayer*, 188).

9. Crossan, *The Greatest Prayer*, 4–8, suggests that the entire biblical tradition of Judaism "flowed through every unit of this prayer" and that the Lord's Prayer exhibits a synonymous parallelism that divides the "you" and the "we" sections, and a crescendo parallelism within each of these sections.

suggest that any study of the prayer must first take into account its sociolinguistic context, since the Lord's Prayer in Matt 6:9–13 is embedded within the larger discourse context of the Sermon on the Mount (Matt 4:17—7:28). As such, I discuss my sociolinguistic methodological approach to the study of the Lord's Prayer in the next section and identify the various sociolinguistic factors in Matt 4:17—7:28 that are tied in to the Lord's Prayer passage. Subsequently, I analyze each of these sociolinguistic factors, from which I simultaneously integrate and respond to these scholars' theological opinions. Then I conclude with a word on the practical application of the Lord's Prayer for the contemporary Christian and church, and the difference it will make if this sociolinguistic context is considered in the study of the Lord's Prayer.

*A Sociolinguistic Methodological Approach to Matthew 6:9–13*

The New Testament is a collection of texts written in a variety of the Greek language of the first-century CE. As such, one of the useful ways of examining this collection of texts is by way of discourse analysis, which "seeks to understand the relationships between language, discourse, and situational context in human communication."[10] From this definition and goal of discourse analysis, I employ two sociolinguistic approaches known as the "ethnography of speaking" and "politeness theory" to describe, analyze, and determine the various social factors in the environment of the communicative process. Ethnography of speaking is a sociolinguistic tool originally developed by Dell Hymes that generally aims at synthesizing the message, form, and context of a speech (or communicative) event.[11] Thus, it is typically con-

---

10. Reed, "Discourse Analysis," 189.
11. For Hymes's summative discussion of this topic, see Hymes, "Ethnography of Speaking." A "speech event" is a series of "speech acts" (a speech act is an instance of speech or utterance that seeks to achieve an objective) in a discourse or conversation within a specific "speech situation" (the entire setting or situation in which people speak, e.g., a party, a church, a classroom, a conference, etc.). For a thorough discussion of speech act, speech

cerned with a systematic and descriptive analysis of the various ways in which people as groups use language (oral or written) to communicate with one another in a specific social and cultural environment.[12] Several ethnographic components are involved in describing a speech event. Hymes's ethnographic framework and formula is a useful and effective tool in describing the various factors involved in a speech event, each of which is intricately interrelated to the others.[13] For my purposes, I describe these various factors according to Hymes's definition of each of these components and Holmes's and Ottenheimer's adaptation of Hymes's ethnographic framework.[14]

*Genre* or type of event: "The notion of genre implies the possibility of identifying formal characteristics traditionally recognized . . . They may occur in (or as) different events."[15]

*Topic* or what people are talking about: this refers to the semantic study of the "lexical hierarchy of the language spoken by a group, including idioms and the content of any conventionalized utterances, for evidence and knowledge of what can be said."[16]

---

event, and speech situation, see Hymes, *Foundations in Sociolinguistics*, 51–53, cf. 101.

12. Cf. Duranti, *Linguistic Anthropology*, 85; Philipsen and Coutu, "Ethnography of Speaking," 355.

13. Since its formulation, Hymes's framework has been widely cited and used by many sociolinguists.

14. See Hymes, *Foundations in Sociolinguistics*, 53–62; Hymes, "Ethnography of Speaking," 110–24; Holmes, *Introduction to Sociolinguistics*, 365–66; Ottenheimer, *Anthropology of Language*, 123–38.

15. Hymes, *Foundations in Sociolinguistics*, 61. Categories such as poem, myth, tale, proverb, riddle, curse, prayer, oration, lecture, commercial, form letter, editorial, phone call, conversation, business meeting, lesson, interview, blog, etc., are meant here.

16. Hymes, "Ethnography of Speaking," 112; examples would be holidays, sport, sociolinguistics, politics, etc. The old rhetorical category of *topoi* can be included here as well.

*Purpose* or *Function*: the reason(s) for the talk: e.g., to plan an event, to catch up socially, to teach something, to persuade someone to help you.

*Key* or emotional tone: e.g., serious, jocular, sarcastic.

*Participants*: who is speaking and who is being spoken to; the characteristics of those present and their relationship: sex, age, social status, role, and role relationship: e.g., mother-daughter, teacher-pupil, TV interviewer, interviewee and audience.

*Message form*: a focus on the syntactic structure: e.g., "He prayed, saying 'God heal him'" (quoting message form) versus "He prayed that he would get well" (reporting contents only).[17]

*Message content* or specific details of what the communication is about: e.g., organizing a time for a football match, describing how a tap works, describing how to make rotis.

After a description of the speech event based on these components, the analysis of the speech event may proceed using the following guideline. Because there is no general rule as to the priority assigned to a particular component, any component may be taken as a starting point for analysis, from which all other components will be viewed in relation to it.[18] It all depends on which component weighs the heaviest. This can be determined based on its function within a speech situation. Whereas for some speech events the rules of speaking may be heavily tied to the participants and setting[19] or to the setting and message con-

---

17. Hymes, *Foundations in Sociolinguistics*, 55. Message form also includes an identification of the code and/or channel: e.g. telephone, letter, email, language and language variety, non-verbal, etc.
18. Ibid., 63.
19. E.g., see the episode in Mark 14:32–42 for Jesus' conversation with three groups of participants (the Eleven, the Three, and the Father) in three different but proximate places.

tent,[20] the Lord's Prayer as a traditionally recognized liturgical hymn or prayer can be primarily bound to its genre, topic, or purpose/function.[21]

Another sociolinguistic tool used in analyzing a communicative event is politeness theory. Being polite is a difficult and complicated business. It involves taking into account the feelings of others, making them feel comfortable, and speaking to them appropriately in light of their relationship to you.[22] This is already discounting the fact that linguistic politeness varies from culture to culture.[23] In sociolinguistic terms, politeness involves an assessment of social relationships based on the social distance and status dimension scales. These dimension scales simultaneously serve as the basis for a distinction between two types of politeness. Positive politeness is solidarity oriented and is therefore assessed using the social distance scale. Because it emphasizes "how well you know someone," it minimizes status differences with the use of more informal expressions (e.g., use of first name) and endearments (e.g., honey, dear, etc.). By contrast, negative politeness is status oriented and therefore engages the status scale. Using "titles," such as Sir, Mr., Mrs., or Dr. to address a conversation partner shows politeness by way of respecting status differences.

With the above two methodological theories in mind, the first step in analyzing the speech event of Matt 6:9–13 is to establish its discourse boundary. Because the Lord's Prayer is a speech/discourse event within a speech/discourse situation (the Sermon on the Mount), the entire discourse situation needs to be analyzed if we are to account for all the social factors and reasons of its occurrence in that speech situation. Its form and function

---

20. E.g., see the episode in Mark 14:53–65, where Jesus appears before the Sanhedrin, the highest Jewish court of justice in Jesus' time, in order to defend himself and pronounce that he is the Son of Man after being coerced to admit that he is the Messiah.
21. Cf. Hymes, *Foundations in Sociolinguistics*, 64–65.
22. Holmes, *Introduction to Sociolinguistics*, 280–81.
23. For a discussion of linguistic politeness in different cultures, see Holmes, *Introduction to Sociolinguistics*, 287–92. Cf. Wardhaugh, *Introduction to Sociolinguistics*, 260–67.

(note the different speech situation in the Lucan passage) can also to a large extent be gleaned from this discourse boundary.

It is generally recognized that Matthew's Gospel is marked by two introductory (4:17; 16:21) and five concluding (7:28; 11:1; 13:53; 19:1; 26:1) formulas that may serve as a structural scheme for analyzing its continuous narrative.[24] This structural outline of the Gospel strongly indicates the literary quality of the Gospel that serves well the purpose of our ethnographic analysis.[25] The introductory junctions at 4:17 and 16:21 seem to clearly demarcate Jesus' public and private ministries respectively. Because the Lord's Prayer is situated within a section commonly known as the Sermon on the Mount (5:1—7:28), the first introductory junction at 4:17 can mark the starting point of our discourse, especially with the narrator's inaugurating remark: "From that time on Jesus began to preach, 'Repent, for the kingdom of heaven has come near.'"[26] With reference to our end point, the concluding formula "When Jesus had finished saying these things, the crowds were amazed at his teaching" at 7:28 is definitely appropriate.

## *A Sociolinguistic Analysis of Matthew 6:9–13*

Having identified this discourse boundary, the various social factors in this speech situation can be described by means of the various ethnographic components I have outlined above.

### *Genre*
There is little doubt, based on the available evidence, that the Lord's Prayer is a liturgical hymn or prayer that has been used by the early church since the Patristic period. There are three earliest extant texts that serve as our sources. The two accounts

---

24. For a survey of the various structural schemes suggested by scholars, see Bauer, *Structure of Matthew's Gospel*. Cf. France, *Matthew: Evangelist and Teacher*, 141–53.
25. Cf. France, *Gospel of Matthew*, 2, 5.
26. Cf. Matt 16:21: "From that time on Jesus began to explain to his disciples that he must go to Jerusalem and suffer many things."

in the Gospels of Matthew and Luke are more familiar to us, but a third one is found in *Didache* 8:2–3.[27] As Crossan also believes, it is arguable that Rom 8:15 and Gal 4:6, as well as Mark 14:36 are our earliest sources for this prayer.[28] On the basis of these sources, there is clear evidence that this prayer was not only used in the liturgy, especially immediately before the Holy Communion, but was also recited exclusively by "baptized" members of the church.[29] Because this prayer was only prayed by baptized members or at the most by baptismal candidates, it was called the "prayer of believers."[30] This genre of the Lord's Prayer suggests that the Lord's Prayer was never used for other purposes except in the liturgy of the church, notably in baptism and communion. Using it as a liturgical hymn or prayer, the church from its earliest beginnings has been reciting it as an act of obedience to the Lord's command "This then is how you should pray" (Matt 6:9) or "When you pray, say" (Luke 11:2), as well as a way of commemorating the Lord's teaching about prayer in its celebration of the sacraments.[31] This is the historical context of the Lord's Prayer in the early church. Thus, any investigation of the prayer's content needs to take this historical context into account.[32]

27. The prayer is introduced by "Do not pray as the hypocrites; but as the Lord commanded in his gospel, thus pray ye," and concluded by a doxology "for thine is the power and the glory forever." Audet, *La Didachè*, 219, dates the *Didache* to as early as 50–70 CE.

28. Cf. Jeremias, *Prayers of Jesus*, 90–91, who suggests that the originality of the Lucan version can also be seen in the brief form of address "*Abba*" in Rom 8:15 and Gal 4:6.

29. This piece of evidence is found in Cyril's twenty-fourth Catechetical Lecture in 350 CE, which is our earliest proof for the liturgical use of the Lord's Prayer in the Mass. See Manson, "The Lord's Prayer." Cf., however, Ayo, *The Lord's Prayer*, 5, who claims that the first reference to the title "Lord's Prayer" is already found in the third-century commentary of Cyprian of Carthage, who, in turn, was indebted to Tertullian.

30. Jeremias, *Prayers of Jesus*, 83.

31. The CEV translates Matt 6:10b as "so that everyone on earth will obey you as you are obeyed in heaven."

32. The various ways in which and reasons for which the ancients prayed the Lord's Prayer seem straightforward. Kirzner, *Art of Jewish Prayer*, 6–7, points out that the Jews believed God could hear the voice of the heart, and

Crossan's suggestion, therefore, that the Lord's Prayer is a revolutionary manifesto and a hymn of hope prayed by Christians for the conscience of the whole world, while a novel one, seems to ignore this historical context. Unlike Crossan, Wilson-Kastner's reflection on the prayer's interconnection with preaching, along with its various pastoral and theological implications for human reality, takes into account this historical context, especially when she acknowledges the prayer's central place in the Sunday worship, Morning Prayer, and the Eucharist. Nonetheless, as noted above, if the Lord's Prayer was originally a liturgical prayer recited by the early church as an act of obedience and to commemorate the Lord's teaching about prayer, it remains uncertain whether interpreting the various components of the prayer is appropriate or necessary, since it is apparent that contemporary interests in interpreting the Lord's Prayer certainly come only as a result of its prominence in the church liturgy.

*Topic*
The Lord's Prayer is embedded in Jesus' teaching about prayer (6:5–15) in the Sermon on the Mount. The central topic in this teaching can be derived from three lexical items that weave this entire section together.[33] The words προσεύχομαι (pray), which

---

they therefore needed to communicate with him spontaneously. In early Judaism, the sixth benediction in the *Amidah* was recited daily: "Forgive us our Father, for we have sinned against thee . . ." (Charlesworth, "Jewish Prayers," 46–47). The petition for bread in Jewish sacred meals was also a common practice even during the time of Jesus: "Blessed art thou, Lord our God, King of the universe, who bringest forth bread from the earth" (Birnbaum, *Daily Prayer Book*, 773–74).

33. A discourse is assumed to have coherence, a linguistic feature that makes a text "hang together." Coherence involves the meaningful relationship of topics or themes, which is determined by cohesion (or cohesive ties): the "set of linguistic resources that every language has for linking one part of the text to another." Westfall, "Blessed Be the Ties That Bind," 204, points out that "the links and bonds formed by cohesive ties create texture in the discourse and contribute to the formation of units and sub-units." In our pericope here, at least two types of cohesive ties/chains are noticeable: (1) lexical chains—formed by the repetition of the same word or cognates; and (2) semantic chains—formed by words that share a common semantic domain. See Halliday and Hasan,

occurs six times (vv. 5, 6, 7, 9), βατταλογέω (speak much/babble; v. 7), πολυλογία (much speaking; v. 7), and αἰτέω (ask/demand; v. 8) are lexical items that belong to the semantic domain "Communication."[34] Whereas προσεύχομαι is classed under the semantic sub-domain "Pray" and αἰτέω under "ask for, request," both βατταλογέω and πολυλογία belong to the sub-domain "speak/talk."[35] It is therefore interesting to note, based on this semantic domain categorization by Louw and Nida, that there is an apparent distinction between the believers' and the hypocrites' prayer and the pagans' mere babble (i.e., talk without meaning). A further distinction can even be made between the believers' sincere and urgent request to God (αἰτέω) and the hypocrites' mere act of praying (προσεύχομαι) to God.[36]

Jesus' introduction to his teaching about prayer in vv. 5–8 is linked to the Lord's Prayer unit at v. 9 by the appropriate form of προσεύχομαι. After telling his disciples about the wrong ways and manner of praying (vv. 5, 7), as well as the right motive and reward of "secret prayer" (v. 8), Jesus begins to teach (or better, to instruct) them to pray (v. 9). The imperative προσεύχεσθε at v. 9, in light of Jesus' teaching about prayer in this context, strongly suggests that he was merely instructing them to pray (though of course not all kinds of prayer would be suitable, so a model is given).[37] The emphasis is on the command to pray, just like the command to fast (6:16–18), to give to the needy (6:1–4), to love one's enemy (5:43–48), etc., and not on the content or *what* to pray, even though there is certainly much to be learned

---

*Language, Context, and Text*, 48, 70–96; Halliday and Hasan, *Cohesion in English*, 4, 274–92. Cf. Brown and Yule, *Discourse Analysis*, 191; Cotterell and Turner, *Linguistics and Biblical Interpretation*, 230–34.

34. See Louw and Nida, *Lexicon*, 1:387.

35. See ibid., 1:398, 408.

36. See ibid., 1:406–8, who point out that αἰτέω, although normally translated as "ask" or "pray," does not mean "pray" in and of itself, but rather, when referring to prayer, is used exclusively of urgent requests made to God.

37. Note that λέγετε in Luke 11:2 (ὅταν προσεύχησθε λέγετε; "whenever you pray, say") is also an imperative.

from the Lord's Prayer itself, as shown in the studies of Crossan and Wilson-Kastner.

The prayer itself is linked together by the terms ἁγιάζω (to hallow/regard as holy; v. 9), ὀφείλημα (debt; v. 12), ὀφειλέτης (debtor; v. 12), and πειρασμός (trial/temptation; v. 13).[38] This unit is joined thematically to the preceding unit through the word ὑποκριτής (hypocrite; v. 5), as all these words are interrelated within the semantic domain "Moral and Ethical Qualities and Related Behavior."[39] Whereas ἁγιάζω is a positive quality (holiness) and appropriately belongs to God, ὀφείλημα, ὀφειλέτης, and πειρασμός (debt, debtor, temptation), which are categorized under the sub-domain "Sin, Wrongdoing, Guilt," and ὑποκριτής (hypocrite), which is classed under the sub-domain "Hypocrisy, Pretense," are negative qualities that concern and are committed by humans. The linguistic relationship of these two groups of lexemes can be considered as a contiguous or antonymous one (words that share some sort of opposition in meaning).[40] As such, in the Lord's Prayer, Jesus may have been primarily concerned with the person's internal attitude towards praying to God (cf. v. 6), in order that debts may not be incurred by and temptations may not overcome the believer.

Crossan, however, tends to see the central topic of the Lord's Prayer as a call for believers to collaborate with God's equity and justice for all humans, as he relates this with the petitions for daily bread and forgiveness of financial debts.[41] His emphasis is on humans as co-heirs with Christ and collaborators with God to make the world conform to the kingdom of justice and righteousness God has established on earth. But as I have shown above, this notion of social, political, and economic collaboration that

---

38. For a discussion of the meaning of the Lord's Prayer based on these thou/thee–we/us divisions, see Ayo, *The Lord's Prayer*, 21–107; Jeremias, *Prayers of Jesus*, 98–107.
39. Louw and Nida, *Lexicon*, 1:741.
40. Antonymous words share at least one semantic feature with each other. They may share a common semantic border but may not overlap each other. See Porter, *Studies in the Greek New Testament*, 72; Silva, *Biblical Words and Their Meaning*, 126.
41. See Crossan, *The Greatest Prayer*, 157–62.

Crossan suggests is far removed from the sociolinguistic context of Jesus' teaching about prayer. The pieces of evidence from the Hebrew biblical tradition that Crossan provides are apparently imposed on the text and context of the Lord's Prayer. Similarly, Wilson-Kastner's emphases on the anthropomorphic and patriarchal language, as well as the transcendence and immanence of God and eschatology are issues that may have concerned neither Jesus nor his disciples.[42] Rather, they are contemporary issues confronting the church today that we hope to address through praying or preaching the Lord's Prayer. Yet the question remains as to whether these things should take precedence over Jesus' emphasis on contrasting the believers' with the hypocrites' and pagans' motive and manner of praying. Needless to say, Jesus might not have been concerned with the issues of anthropomorphism and patriarchy as we would have it today.[43]

*Purpose*

There are four instances in this discourse situation that point toward the purpose of the Lord's Prayer, that is, why it was embedded in the Sermon on the Mount narrative or why Jesus included it in his teaching about prayer. This purpose traces back to 4:17, the inauguration of Jesus' preaching ministry; 4:23, his teaching ministry in the synagogues of Galilee; and 5:2, his sermon on various topics on the Mount, all of which suggest that the purpose of the Lord's Prayer is a function of or is derived from Jesus' teaching on prayer. This fact is important, since the stress of Jesus' teaching is on the command to pray and the attitude in prayer;[44] the content of the prayer, if it has a specific

---

42. Wilson-Kastner, "Pastoral Theology," 112–13, 115–16.

43. Likewise, John Calvin believes that the Lord's Prayer is Jesus' own prayer. He emphasizes the manner in which one should pray and the importance of inward and spiritual prayer before discussing its content. For him, the Lord's Prayer, which is a model for all right prayer, is both a private conversation and communal praise (Calvin, *Institutes*, 73–75). For a summary of Calvin's explanation of the first and second triple petitions in the Lord's Prayer, see McKee, "John Calvin's Teaching," 93, 97–105.

44. Ancient Jews seem to have prayed three times a day (Dan 6:10; cf. Acts 3:1; 10:30) in various postures: standing (cf. Mark 11:25; Luke 18:11, 13;

purpose or meaning, is largely contingent on the reader or interpreter and therefore must always be attached to this purpose. For Crossan, the purposes of the Lord's Prayer are for "the conscience of the whole world" and to give "hope for all humanity." The vagueness of these purposes is not only couched in the language style and vocabulary used, but is also primarily seen in its congruence with the content of the Lord's Prayer. Yes, the Lord's Prayer can be a hymn of hope for the Christian who has a personal relationship with and trust in God. But is it a hope for the conscience of the whole world? In order to argue for this, we have to impose our own meaning on it, since this is not its purpose in the context of Jesus' teaching about prayer. A teaching that is focused on the command and attitude to prayer has personal or spiritual transformation and not some external or judicial practices as its goal.[45] Wilson-Kastner, on the other hand, recognizes Jesus' *Abba* address as showing Jesus' intimacy with the Father, from which his disciples are to learn, and emulate this same kind of intimacy with and dependence on the Father.[46] The problem, however, is with her claim that the Lord's Prayer offers hope of rescuing the world as people realize that they all belong to one family with a common Father.[47] This claim resembles that of Crossan's "hope for all humanity," which I think is not within Jesus' intended purpose in the prayer.

---

1 Tim 2:8), kneeling (2 Chr 6:13; Ps 95:6; Luke 22:41), or prostrate (Num 16:22; Matt 26:39). See Luz, *Matthew 1–7*, 359, who argues that Jews prayed at intermittent times; and Morris, *Matthew*, 140, who insists that they prayed at specific times.

45. For instance, the same Lord who taught this prayer also said, "do not call anyone on earth 'father,' for you have one Father who is in heaven" (Matt 23:9). Jeremias, *The Lord's Prayer*, 63, points out that Jesus in Matt 23:9 forbids his disciples to use the *Abba* address in everyday language as a courtesy title. They are to use it exclusively for God. Similarly, Tittle, *The Lord's Prayer*, 13, writes, "Simply to say that God is our father is not enough"; we are to conform to his image and likeness.

46. In Jesus' historical and social context, the father figure symbolized the head and provider of the family (Wilson-Kastner, "Pastoral Theology," 113–15).

47. Ibid., 121–22.

Second, although Crossan recognizes the anthropomorphism (and patriarchal imagery) in the Lord's Prayer, he nonetheless rejects an exclusive use of the term "Father in Heaven"; instead, he wants to call God "Householder of Earth."[48] But I think that seeing God as the householder of earth has its proper place in a different context (e.g., Ps 24:1; Col 1:15–20). Moreover, as Wilson-Kastner rightly points out, patriarchy and anthropomorphism must be distinguished. On the one hand, "How dare we encourage others to call God Father and thus perpetrate the negative effects of patriarchy?"[49] But on the other hand, because the word "Father," whether we like it or not, resonates deeply with our familial, social, and religious relationships, we can "escape neither the profundity of the feelings nor the responsibility of preaching about God as 'Abba, Father'."[50] The Father is a God who wills intimacy with us. Jesus also wills the intimate character of his disciples' relationship with God; he was not concerned with masculinity or femininity in God.[51] This intimacy is evident in God giving us bread, forgiving us our sins, and delivering us from evil.

## Participants

The participants in this discourse situation should be distinguished from the participants in the Lord's Prayer pericope. As most studies on the Lord's Prayer demonstrate, the participants in the prayer itself, ὑμεῖς (you, plural) and ἡμῶν (us, plural); πατήρ ἡμῶν (our father); ὀφειλέτης (debtor); τοῦ πονηροῦ (the evil one), are the ones that need to be studied. But as I have pointed out above, this is perhaps only a secondary purpose in the context of Jesus' teaching about prayer. What is important here is to determine who the real audiences of Jesus were in this episode. On the one hand, there are the ὄχλοι (crowds; 5:1; 7:28), and on the other hand, there are the μαθηταί (disciples; 5:1).

---

48. Crossan, *The Greatest Prayer*, 35–41, esp. 35, 41.
49. Wilson-Kastner, "Pastoral Theology," 113.
50. Ibid., 114.
51. Ibid., 119–21. Cf. Jeremias, *The Lord's Prayer*, 17–21.

Based on the words of 5:1–2, "his disciples came to him and, opening his mouth, he began to teach them," it can be deduced that Jesus began to teach the beatitudes only to his disciples. Nevertheless, as groups began to arrive and settle down, the crowd grew larger and larger, such that at the end of his sermon, the narrator remarks: "When Jesus had finished saying these things, the crowds were amazed at his teaching" (7:28). Whether other people had heard his teaching on prayer is irrelevant; the key thing to note is that Jesus most likely intended his sermon for his disciples.

Analyzing the Lord's Prayer based on its intended audience can radically affect how we interpret the content of the Lord's Prayer. It seems unlikely that the Lord's Prayer is "a prayer from the heart of Judaism on the lips of Christianity for the conscience of the world."[52] Rather, the Lord's Prayer is Jesus' teaching about praying (an appropriate prayer) both for Jewish Christians and other Christians alike as they seek to communicate with their heavenly Father. Wilson–Kastner supports this point, although I am not entirely sure how to take her assertion that the Lord's Prayer also speaks about human freedom and responsibility as God empowers and liberates us through our relationship with him.

Prayer is more than a verbal act. It embraces and accompanies the entire dimension of human existence before God.[53] Jesus acted on what he had taught his disciples in the Lord's Prayer.[54] Christians, even though perhaps unreflectively shortsighted, recite the Lord's Prayer in loving obedience to this teaching to converse with the Father and to give him continuous honor and praise (vv. 9, 13b).[55]

---

52. Crossan, *The Greatest Prayer*, 2, 182.
53. Lochman, "The Lord's Prayer in Our Time," 8.
54. Thielicke, *Prayer That Spans the World*, 23, argues that "everything that he [Jesus] does is the reflection, the *reverberation of that heart*."
55. Some late manuscripts end with "for yours is the kingdom and the power and the glory forever" at v. 13. Although perhaps overly stated, in one of his sermons, Thielicke asserts that "Jesus himself had no intention whatsoever of being the "Son of God," [or in Crossan's term, Heir of God] but wished only

*Key, Message Form, and Message Content*
The following elements, key, message form, and message content are all tightly related. In what follows, therefore, I will treat my analysis of these three components together.

*Key.* The emotional tone of the prayer is significant in our analysis, inasmuch as it is important for determining its topic and purpose. It may help us understand whether the Lord's Prayer continues naturally with Jesus' introduction about prayer in 6:5–8. It can be argued that the prayer itself is characterized by an earnest request or petition by children to their father. On the one hand, "Our Father," regardless of how we want to interpret it, definitely sounds like there is an intimate relationship when it is uttered by children to their father.[56] One can observe that the address "Our Father" demonstrates a status difference (negative politeness) between God and his children. On the other hand, the eight out of nine verbal imperatives characterize the "petitionary" tone of the prayer. Even the only subjunctive verb μὴ εἰσενέγκῃς ἡμᾶς (lead us not into) at v. 13 is used as an imperative.[57] Both the familial and the petitionary tone of the prayer are tied in to Jesus' teaching that "your Father knows what you need before you ask him" (v. 8).

*Message Form.* Jesus' introduction, "Therefore pray this way," to the prayer may indicate that the prayer is an embedded unit within Jesus' teaching about prayer in 6:5–15. In other words, he may have been excerpting a "message form" and not

---

to reveal the Father more clearly while he himself remained unrecognized in the background" (Thielicke, *Prayer That Spans the World*, 22, cf. 156).

56. The "*Abba* Father" address in Rom 8:15 and Gal 4:6, and especially in Jesus' passionate prayer in Mark 14:36, all illustrate this intimately familial language. For an excellent discussion on this issue, see Jeremias, *Prayers of Jesus*, 54–65. Cf. Juel, "The Lord's Prayer," 61–62; Crossan, *The Greatest Prayer*, 31–41.

57. Porter, *Idioms*, 56, points out that the "aorist imperative is restricted in its usage in prohibitions. Instead, the negated (with μή) aorist subjunctive serves to express prohibition in the second person, even though the negated aorist imperative usually is used in the third person . . . The use of the negated aorist subjunctive as a prohibition is very widespread."

reporting or teaching the contents of the prayer. Even if we may speculate that the prayer is Jesus' way of praying to the Father as remembered by his contemporaries through the familiar "*Abba* Father" address, it is equally possible that he is merely quoting his own *Abba* Father "message form" here.[58]

*Message Content.* As already noted above, exclusively examining the content of the Lord's Prayer is a highly subjective and reader-contingent endeavor. One evidence of this is the massive literature that has been produced so far, which reduces the possibility of knowing which one comes closest to Jesus' intended meaning, including Crossan's and Wilson-Kastner's proposals. The best we can offer is to say that the Lord's Prayer contains some of the essential components of the kind(s) of prayer(s) Jesus wants us to include in our daily prayers. Of course, both the Old and New Testaments have many examples of the various forms and kinds of prayers that we can emulate and study.[59]

In sum, based on these three sociolinguistic components, it is fair to argue that Jesus might have merely cited his typical form of prayer that is characterized by a language of petition or request, in order to instruct his disciples to pray (a suitable prayer). Our prayer may or may not contain the exact components of this prayer, since we find many other forms of prayers in Scripture.

The nonviolent God who distributes equity and justice to the world that Crossan finds in the Lord's Prayer, therefore, is not featured in the Lord's Prayer. The contrast that he makes between the distributive justice of the nonviolent God and the retributive justice of the violent God of the Old Testament is one that has been claimed since the time of Marcion in the second century CE. Consequently, his question whether the teacher of this prayer is a representative of violence or nonviolence is out

---

58. For a good discussion of the various positions on this issue, see Evans, *Mark 8:27—16:20*, 412–13.

59. Greenberg, *Biblical Prose Prayer*, 59–60, lists ninety-seven prose texts where words of prayers are embedded within the narrative contexts of the Hebrew Scriptures.

of place. Similarly, the question whether God is calling for human collaboration in the prayer is hard to answer; neither the form nor the content nor the tone of the prayer elicits such a notion or concern. That there is an eschatological tone in the phrases "Hallowed be your name. Your kingdom come, your will be done," is perhaps the best we can say here. As Wilson-Kastner suggests, this phrase calls for human participation in a cosmic drama.

One final word needs to be said as to Crossan's main contention that God should be thought of as the "householder" in the Lord's Prayer. To this end, I refer to the episode of Jesus' *Abba* prayer in Gethsemane. In Mark 14:32–36, Jesus' conversation with the Father is both highly intimate (see the emphatic πάτερ μου, my Father, in Matt 26:39)[60] and status sensitive (features a superior-subordinate relationship).[61] Jesus demonstrates solidarity (positive politeness) with the Father by submitting to his Father's will (v. 36). At the same time, the episode also shows status difference (negative politeness), when Jesus kneels down and confidently cries out, "Abba, Father, everything is possible for you" (v. 35).[62] This convergence of both positive and negative politeness is perhaps unique and may not happen in human situations.[63] At the cross, the separation between the Father and the Son, if indeed there was one, was only momentary (Ps 22:1; Matt 27:46). Shriver notes that when the early Christians uttered the word *Abba*, it embodied fully the good news that nothing

---

60. Cf. the use of the vocative here, as well as in Matt 26:41–42, with the simple "Father" in Matt 11:25–26.

61. The word Αββα "combines aspects of supernatural authority and care for his people" (Louw and Nida, *Lexicon*, 1:139).

62. There is no evidence in pre-Christian Palestinian Judaism that God was ever addressed as *Abba* by a Jew in prayer (Ashton, "Abba," 1:7). For a good discussion of the uniqueness and significance of the title "Father" in the teachings of Jesus, see Stein, *Method and Message of Jesus' Teachings*, 82–89.

63. Responding to J. Heinemann's comment that there is no special importance to the fact that God is addressed as "Father" or as "Our Father" in the Lord's Prayer, since "Master" or "God" are likewise often used in Jewish prayers, Juel cites statistical evidence from the Gospels and argues that based on such statistics, "reference to God as 'Father' is uncommon and noteworthy" (Juel, "The Lord's Prayer," 59–60).

could separate them from the love of God (Rom 8:39), a claim that neither Wilson-Kastner nor I would deny.[64]

## Conclusion

In this study and my dialogue with Wilson-Kastner and Crossan I have highlighted the various points of disagreement (and agreement) between my sociolinguistic analysis and these scholars' interpretation of the Lord's Prayer. I have also shown in various instances why several of their proposals might be unlikely or implausible.

The Lord's Prayer, I firmly believe, is both Jesus' prayer and his teaching about prayer. Therefore, it has both personal and social dimensions to it. These dimensions are the exact places in the human realm where the Lord's Prayer should be applied, but one needs to be circumspect in this endeavor and should interpret the prayer within its sociolinguistic context. The personal dimension of the prayer can be gleaned from Jesus' embodiment of his passionate communion with God (Matt 6:9; Mark 14:36; John 17), as well as his emphasis on solitude and quietness in praying (Matt 6:5–6; Mark 1:35; Luke 5:16). He finds his strength and power through prayer (Matt 4:10; Mark 14:36). The social dimension of the prayer can be found in Jesus' teachings about prayer like the Lord's Prayer. He taught about prayer because he came from a people who also taught him to pray.[65]

From his ancestral background Jesus must have envisioned that all his brothers and sisters would corporately pray whenever they gathered together as a community. The Lord's Prayer serves this particular purpose for Jesus' new community.

For this reason, though I have nothing against those who wish to interpret the Lord's Prayer for contemporary practical, theo-

---

64. Shriver, *The Lord's Prayer*, 16.
65. The Old Testament assumes prayer (cf. 1 Kings 8) and has exhortations to pray (e.g., Ps 32:6; Isa 55:6; Jer 29:11–14) and many examples of prayer (e.g., Neh 1:5–10). Jews of Jesus' day had regular prayer times (Luke 1:10; Acts 3:1). For a discussion of first-century Jewish prayer practice as relates to the Lord's Prayer, see Kistemaker, "The Lord's Prayer in the First Century."

logical, and ecclesiastical purposes, I nonetheless think that we ought to take the prayer's sociolinguistic context seriously. Otherwise, all kinds of interpretations can be made in our study of the prayer, especially when we want to use the prayer for our own purposes. But it is precisely at this juncture that the true meaning and original purpose of the prayer can be lost. And this is manifested clearly in both Wilson-Kastner's and Crossan's study of the prayer. I fail to see in their studies the important contrast between the believers' and the hypocrites' and pagans' manner of praying that highlights Jesus' teaching about the right motive and manner in praying. Neither of them has emphasized Jesus' simple but urgent command to pray (a suitable prayer), inasmuch as they would perhaps stress the command to give to the needy and to fast if they were to study the pericopes preceding and following the Lord's Prayer, as well as the other topics in the Sermon on the Mount.

Finally, what difference will it make if we incorporate this sociolinguistic context into our study? The answer to this question, I think, is clear based on the result of this study. I can see that our analysis and interpretation of the Lord's Prayer will shift from merely analyzing the various components of the prayer to emphasizing the motive and manner Jesus wants from us whenever we pray (especially the Lord's Prayer).

## Bibliography

Ashton, John. "Abba." In *The Anchor Bible Dictionary*, edited by D. N. Freedman, 1:7–8. 6 vols. New York; Doubleday, 1992.

Audet, Jean Paul. *La Didachè: Instructions des Apôtres*. Études Bibliques. Paris: J. Gabalda, 1958.

Ayo, Nicholas. *The Lord's Prayer: A Survey Theological and Literary*. London: University of Notre Dame Press, 1992.

Bauer, D. R. *The Structure of Matthew's Gospel: A Study in Literary Design*. JSNTS 31. Sheffield: Almond, 1988.

Baugh, John, and Joel Sherzer, eds. *Language in Use: Readings in Sociolinguistics*. Englewood Cliffs: Prentice-Hall, 1984.

Birnbaum, Philip. *Daily Prayer Book: Ha-Siddur Ha-Shalem*. New York: Hebrew Publishing, 1995.

Brooke, George J. "The Lord's Prayer Interpreted through John and Paul." *Downside Review* 98 (1980) 298–311.

Brown, Gillian, and George Yule. *Discourse Analysis*. Cambridge Textbooks in Linguistics. Cambridge: Cambridge University Press, 1983.

Calvin, John. *Institutes of the Christian Religion* (1936 ed.). Translated by Ford Lewis Battles. Rev. ed. Grand Rapids: Eerdmans, 1989.

Charlesworth, James H. "Jewish Prayers in the Time of Jesus." In *The Lord's Prayer: Perspectives for Reclaiming Christian Prayer*, edited by Daniel L. Migliore, 36–55. Grand Rapids: Eerdmans, 1993.

Chase, Frederick. *The Lord's Prayer in the Early Church*. Cambridge: Cambridge University Press, 1891. Reprint, Nendeln, Liechtenstein: Krause, 1967.

Cotterell, Peter, and Max Turner. *Linguistics and Biblical Interpretation*. Downers Grove, IL: InterVarsity, 1989.

Crossan, John Dominic. *The Greatest Prayer: Rediscovering the Revolutionary Message of the Lord's Prayer*. New York: HarperOne, 2010.

Duranti, Alessandro. *Linguistic Anthropology.* Cambridge Textbooks in Linguistics. Cambridge: Cambridge University Press, 1997.

Evans, Craig A. *Mark 8:27—16:20.* WBC 34B. Nashville: Thomas Nelson, 2001.

France, R. T. *The Gospel of Matthew.* NICNT. Grand Rapids: Eerdmans, 2007.

———. *Matthew: Evangelist and Teacher.* Exeter, UK: Paternoster, 1989.

Greenberg, Moshe. *Biblical Prose Prayer as a Window to the Popular Religion of Ancient Israel.* Los Angeles: University of California Press, 1983.

Halliday, M. A. K., and Ruqaiya Hasan. *Cohesion in English.* Harlow: Longman, 1976.

———. *Language, Context and Text: Aspects of Language in a Social-Semiotic Perspective.* Oxford: Oxford University Press, 1989.

Holmes, Janet. *An Introduction to Sociolinguistics.* 3rd ed. Harlow: Pearson & Longman, 2008.

Hymes, Dell. *Foundations in Sociolinguistics: An Ethnographic Approach.* Philadelphia: University of Pennsylvania Press, 1974.

———. "The Ethnography of Speaking." In *Readings in the Sociology of Language*, edited by Joshua A. Fishman, 99–138. The Hague: Mouton, 1970.

Jeremias, Joachim. *The Lord's Prayer* Translated by John Reumann. Philadelphia: Fortress, 1969.

———. *The Prayers of Jesus*. Studies in Biblical Theology 6. London: SCM, 1967.

Juel, Donald. "The Lord's Prayer in the Gospels of Matthew and Luke." In *The Lord's Prayer: Perspectives for Reclaiming Christian Prayer*, edited by Daniel L. Migliore, 56–70. Grand Rapids: Eerdmans, 1993.

Kirzner, Yitzchok. *The Art of Jewish Prayer*. Lanham, MD: Jason Aronson, 1991.

Kistemaker, Simon J. "The Lord's Prayer in the First Century." *JETS* 21 (1998) 323–28.

Lochman, Jan Milič. "The Lord's Prayer in Our Time: Praying and Drumming. In *The Lord's Prayer: Perspectives for Reclaiming Christian Prayer*, edited by Daniel L. Migliore, 5–19. Grand Rapids: Eerdmans, 1993.

Louw, Johannes P., and Eugene A. Nida. *Greek-English Lexicon of the New Testament: Based on Semantic Domains*. 2nd ed. 2 vols. New York: UBS, 1989.

Luz, Ulrich. *Matthew 1–7: A Commentary*. Minneapolis: Fortress, 1989.

Manson, T. W. "The Lord's Prayer." *BJRL* 38 (1955–56) 99–113, 436–48.

Marty, Martin. *The Hidden Discipline*. St. Louis: Concordia, 1962.

McKee, Elsie Anne. "John Calvin's Teaching on the Lord's Prayer." In *The Lord's Prayer: Perspectives for Reclaiming Christian Prayer*, edited by Daniel L. Migliore, 88–106. Grand Rapids: Eerdmans, 1993.

Morris, Leon. *The Gospel according to Matthew*. Pillar New Testament Commentary. Grand Rapids: Eerdmans, 1992.

Ottenheimer, Harriet. *The Anthropology of Language: An Introduction to Linguistic Anthropology*. 2nd ed. Belmont, CA: Wadsworth, 2009.

Palmer, George H. *The Lord's Prayer*. Chicago: Pilgrim, 1932.

Philipsen, Gerry, and Lisa M. Coutu. "The Ethnography of Speaking." In *Handbook of Language and Social Interaction*, edited by Kristine L. Fitch and Robert E. Sanders, 355–79. Mahwah, NJ: Lawrence Erlbaum, 2005.

Porter, Stanley E. *Idioms of the Greek of the New Testament*. 2nd ed. Biblical Languages: Greek 2. Sheffield: Sheffield Academic, 1999.

———. *Studies in the Greek New Testament: Theory and Practice*. Studies in Biblical Greek 6. New York: Peter Lang, 1996.

———. "Translations of the Bible (since the KJV)." In *Dictionary of Biblical Criticism and Interpretation*, edited by Stanley E. Porter, 362–68. London: Routledge, 2009.

Reed, Jeffrey T. "Discourse Analysis." In *Handbook to Exegesis of the New Testament*, edited by Stanley E. Porter, 189–217. Leiden: Brill, 1997.

Reyman, Leslie. "Finding Aid for Patricia Wilson-Kastner Papers, 1944–1998." Pages 1–24. Online: http://library.columbia.edu/content/dam/libraryweb/libraries/burke/fa/awts/ldpd_5635472.pdf.

Shriver, Donald W. *The Lord's Prayer: A Way of Life*. Louisville: John Knox, 1983.

Silva, Moisés. *Biblical Words and Their Meaning: An Introduction to Lexical Semantics*. Rev. ed. Grand Rapids: Zondervan, 1994.

Stein, Robert H. *The Method and Message of Jesus' Teachings*. Louisville: John Knox, 1994.

Thielicke, Helmut. *The Prayer That Spans the World: Sermons on the Lord's Prayer*. Translated by John W. Doberstein. London: James Clark, 1965.

Tittle, Ernest Freemont. *The Lord's Prayer*. New York: Abingdon-Cokesbury, 1942.

Walker, William O., Jr. "The Lord's Prayer in Matthew and in John." *NTS* 28 (1982) 237–56.

Wardhaugh, Ronald. *An Introduction to Sociolinguistics*. 5th ed. Blackwell Textbooks in Linguistics. Malden, MA: Blackwell, 2006.

Westfall, Cynthia Long. "Blest Be the Ties That Bind: Semantic Domains and Cohesive Chains in Hebrews 1.1—2.4 and 12.5–8." *JGRChJ* 6 (2009) 199–216.

Wilson-Kastner, Patricia. "Pastoral Theology and the Lord's Prayer: We Dare to Pray." In *The Lord's Prayer: Perspectives for Reclaiming Christian Prayer*, edited by Daniel L. Migliore, 107–24. Grand Rapids: Eerdmans, 1993.

AN EMPOWERED PEOPLE:
A LITERARY READING OF 1 KINGS 12:1–20

Kojo Okyere
University of Cape Coast, Ghana

*Introduction*

After the death of Solomon, the united monarchy fell apart into two divisions; the northern kingdom (Israel) and the southern kingdom (Judah). This fate is interpreted theologically as Yahweh's punishment for Solomon's crimes, which included the establishment of idolatrous worship (cf. 1 Kgs 11:31–33).[1] Organ, however, points out that a careful examination of the narrative shows that Rehoboam is responsible for the division.[2] Accordingly, many scholars believe that as the story stands, it is Rehoboam's intransigence and foolishness that led to the division of the kingdom.[3] The role played by the Israelites themselves in their secession, surprisingly, has not been acknowledged. Although the popular view blaming Rehoboam's intransigence and foolishness is to a large extent valid, it is not the complete story. An important part of the story is not told. Indeed the theological explanations in the narrative point to Yahweh as the one behind the turn of events (cf. 1 Kgs 12:15). Nonetheless, underneath these theological colorings are the actions and desires

---

1. That there was a theological basis for the division of the monarchy is supported by Solomon's sin, Ahijah's prophecy about the division, and prophet Shemaiah's message that what happened was God's will. The Deuteronomist used these theological contexts to explain that what happened did not happen by chance; rather God was at work in the tragic division of the nation. See Anderson, *Living Word of the Old Testament*, 232–33.
2. See Organ, "The Man Who Would Be King."
3. Devries, *1 Kings*, 158–59.

of the human characters.[4] If the human characters and their actions are brought to the fore, it becomes clear that Rehoboam's intransigence and foolishness do not fully account for the division. Lying latently in this fated development is the role played by the Israelites and their leader Jeroboam. First Kings 12:1–20,[5] when considered carefully, provides enough evidence to support this reading.

Acknowledging the role of the Israelites in the division is important. Their actions resonate with a number of contemporary happenings. All over the world, ordinary people are discovering their voices: they stand up against their governments and other powerful institutions. The wondrous case of the Arab Spring, particularly, comes to mind. The disgruntled Arabs believe that for a long time they have been "marginalized" in political decisions as well as in social and economic decisions.[6] The ability of marginalized people to identify their problems and map out strategies to solve them is termed "empowerment." The concept of empowerment reveals an inherent human potential that can be harnessed for the good of society. This paper reads the story of Israel's secession from the united monarchy from the perspective

---

4. Even though it seems that the author of Kings tried to put the historical context of the division under the theological carpet, the northerners in their encounter with Rehoboam exposed this historical context. Nothing in their protest against Solomon's harsh policy points to a theological reason. What this means is that even when the theological reasons are relegated to the background, the division of the monarchy can still be understood.

5. First Kings 12:1–20 is part of the Deuteronomistic History. In its final form, this text emerged from Judah. However, McEntire, *Blood of Abel*, 93 n. 2, indicates that although the Deuteronomistic History was composed in Judah, 1 Kgs 12:1–20 is sympathetic to northern concerns. DeVries, *1 Kings*, 157, also argues that a Judahite wrote the story but the author was conciliatory in tone. The narrative most probably is southern in origin, however, Rehoboam, and not the northerners, receives the blame for the secession. This suggests that the action of the northerners is legitimized by the narrator. However, the northerners have not been the main subject of study for the narrative, despite the extensive discussions on the text.

6. Pollack, "Introduction," 2–3.

of the concept of empowerment.[7] By approaching the text from this perspective, we gain greater insight into the role played by the northern tribes in determining their fate. Not only that, we make the biblical story gain contemporary relevance, as we explore how the text and the modern experience illuminate each other.

## *Empowerment*

The concept of empowerment is not a topic natural to the study of ancient Israel, nor has it been used for other societies prior to the twentieth century. The emergence and growth of this concept is a natural reaction to the ever-changing times in the political, social, and developmental spheres of human life. However, the principles and assumptions underlying these concepts have existed, although in an elementary form, in many pre-modern civilizations. For instance, a system of popular government can be traced among African societies, especially within the institution of chieftaincy.[8] Knight also points out the rudimentary form of the concept of human rights in ancient Israel.[9] Thus if empowerment is today an important issue, one that is central to the fate of humanity, then the pre-modern world is not to be merely eliminated from the discussion. A journey into ancient cultures to examine traces of empowerment will increase our appreciation of the development of the concept. However, before we examine how 1 Kgs 12:1–20 reflects the concept of empowerment, we need first to understand what "empowerment" is.

The term "empowerment" is difficult to pin down. As a construct, the concept of empowerment is shared by many disciplines such as community development, education, economics, psychology, and the study of social movements and organizations. It has also become a term people take for granted,

---

7. The text will be read synchronically, thus much attention will not be given to historical-critical matters unless they are necessary to the argument.

8. Gyekye, *African Cultural Values*, 110, explains that foreigners and travelers during pre-colonial and colonial times testified to the role ordinary people played in Africa's political systems.

9. Knight, "Political Rights."

comfortable and unquestioned, something that very different institutions and practices seem to be able to agree upon. For instance, it is the mantra of development practitioners and theorists—the unquestioned 'good' aspired to by such diverse institutions as the World Bank, Oxfam, and the most radical non-government organizations. Thus Rappaport notes that it is easier to define the term in absence than in practice.[10] Similarly, Zimmerman describes the concept as enigmatic.[11]

Despite this difficulty, some scholars have provided useful definitions. For example, Narayan-Parkeer defines empowerment as the "expansion of assets and capabilities of poor people to participate in, negotiate with, influence, control, and hold accountable institutions that affect their lives."[12] Petesch, Smulovitz, and Walton hold a similar view when they define empowerment as a process through which disadvantaged communities or people make purposeful choices as a response to their poor state of living.[13] Sadan, on her part, conceptualizes empowerment as a "transition from a state of powerlessness to a state of more control over one's life, fate, and environment."[14] These definitions capture the concept as a multi-dimensional social, psychological, and political process that helps people gain control over their lives. Thus empowerment recognizes people's ability to set their own agenda to make their life worth living. To be empowered is to gain a sense of dignity, make decisions, and take responsibility associated with the decisions.

Central to empowerment is the concept of power and power relations.[15] To empower implies the ability of the empowered to exert power over or to make things happen. As an action verb, empower suggests giving the ability to change the world, to overcome opposition. It has a transformatory sound, an implicit promise of change, often for the better. Thus a deeper under-

---

10. Rappaport, "Studies in Empowerment," 2.
11. Zimmerman, "Taking Aim on Empowerment Research," 169.
12. Narayan-Parkeer, *Empowerment and Poverty Reduction*, xviii.
13. Petesch et al., "Evaluating Empowerment," 40–41.
14. Sadan, *Empowerment and Community Planning*, 13.
15. Ibid., 33.

standing of power will make possible a better appreciation of states of powerlessness, and the processes by which individuals or groups struggle for control over their lives and environments. The concept of participation is also integral to the empowerment process. Participation promotes the need for people to be in the know and be involved in issues concerning their lives. In other words, people's ability to partake in decision making is crucial to changing their lives. Clearly then, the empowerment process targets the marginalized or the powerless. It allows these groups of people greater freedom, autonomy, and control over their responsibility for decision making.

## Solomon and the Northerners

According to empowerment theorists, the point of departure in the empowerment process is a state of human misery, which can be termed "powerlessness," "oppression," or "deprivation." This state is referred to as a "position."[16] The need to identify the nature of an individual's or a group's "position" is important to the empowerment process. Rappaport argues that powerlessness is an attitude that results from the incorporation of past experiences, ongoing behavior, and continued patterns of thinking that are embedded and reproduced by inequitable power relations.[17] Thus the encounter between Rehoboam and "all Israel," can be better appreciated when we look at the larger context of their encounter.[18] Also, we need to determine the "position" of "all Israel" in order to appreciate the nature of the exchanges that transpired between the two. The institution of monarchy pro-

---

16. Carr, "Rethinking Empowerment Theory," 13.
17. Rappaport, "Studies in Empowerment," 3–5.
18. First Kings 12:1–20 is part of the larger pericope identified as the Jeroboam Story (1 Kgs 11:26—14:20). See Walsh, *Old Testament Narrative*, 10. However, the narrative of 1 Kgs 12:1–20 demands a much larger context if we are to understand the turn of events. This is because the slogan chanted by "all Israel" in v. 16 points to David's role, however remote, in the division. Again, the request by "all Israel" accused Solomon for the harsh policies against the north.

vides the framework for analyzing the power relations between the two sides.

An understanding of the exact political organization of the Israelites before their adoption of the institution of monarchy has been elusive to scholars.[19] However, what is known is that various tribes did have a common sense of identity through their religious tradition, although they sometimes operated independently of each other.[20] The adoption of monarchy gradually changed this pre-monarchic loose confederation into that of a state. One dominant feature of this change, which anti-monarchic elements were quick to point out, was the tension in the institution of kingship in relation to the loss of freedom and the lack of justice (cf. 1 Samuel 8). The reign of the first king, Saul, saw little of this tension. During the reign of David, the tensions began to emerge (his last years could be termed despotic).[21] It was Solomon, however, as many scholars posit, who served as the inspiration for the scathing warning against kingship in the popular anti-monarchy speech by Samuel. According to Cross, Solomon set out to establish an imperial rule. He explains further: "while David eschewed outright innovations which seriously violated traditional religious and social institutions, his son Solomon sought to transfer Israel into a full-fledged Oriental monarchy and was prepared to ignore or to flout older institutions in his determination to centralize powers and to consolidate his realm."[22]

Solomon's innovations included the division of his kingdom into districts and elaborate building projects. With his imperial intentions, Solomon had to devise ways to have the necessary funds and labor to carry out his ambitions. In 1 Kgs 4:7–19 we read about the division of the state into tax districts. Eleven of these divisions were in the northern regions while only one was

---

19. See Hayes, "Period of the Judges," 307.
20. The traditions in the book of Judges show the independence of the tribes and the occasional rivalry between some tribes; see ibid., 322.
21. See Donner, "Separate States of Israel and Judah," 384.
22. Cross, *Canaanite Myth*, 241.

in the south.²³ This, to any cursory observation, is an obvious attempt to demand more from a particular section of the society. In 1 Kgs 9:21 it is reported that Solomon used the subjects of the neighboring states as the labor for his projects. It appears, however, that Solomon's attempt to restrict the forced labor to foreigners proved inadequate, and he had to resort to his own people to supplement labor for the tasks needed to complete his projects (1 Kgs 5:27–32). The text reads that "all Israel" was forcibly taxed, which implies that Judah would be included in this. However, as Sweeney argues, it is not out of the way to believe that the forced labor was made up of men from the northern tribes.²⁴ Soggin concurs with this view when he writes, "Israel, and not Judah . . . was subjected to services it considered a grievous infringement of its liberties."²⁵ This suggestion is supported by the reading in 1 Kgs 11:28 that says that Jeroboam[26] was in charge of the forced labor of the "house of Joseph."²⁷ Another case of Solomon's discrimination against the northern tribes was his ceding of the Galilean cities to Hiram when Solomon was unable to redeem his debt (cf. 1 Kgs 9:10–14).²⁸ Thus Finkelstein and Silberman write: "the northern tribes are depicted in 1 Kings as being treated like little more than colonial subjects by David's son Solomon."²⁹

With the adoption of monarchy, ancient Israel had its balance of power shift radically in favor of the king, whose legitimacy

---

23. Sweeney, "Critique of Solomon," 614–15.

24. Sweeney bases his argument on the fact that "the corvee in Lebanon would suggest that, for logistical reasons, the majority of the laborers came from the northern tribes" (ibid., 614).

25. Soggin, "Davidic-Solomonic Kingdom," 378.

26. The presence of Jeroboam is important to note at this juncture. As evident from the narrative that follows (11:26—14:20), he is a central figure in the plot, helping shape the fate of the northerners; see Walsh, *Old Testament Narrative*, 29; see also Long, *1 Kings*, 131.

27. The phrase "house of Joseph" is used to refer to the northern tribes of Ephraim, Manasseh, and Benjamin. See Hayes, *Introduction to the Bible*, 77.

28. Sweeney, "Critique of Solomon," 614–15; Halpern also details the effect of Solomon's action on the northerners ("Sectionalism and the Schism," 519–32).

29. Finkelstein and Silberman, *Bible Unearthed*, 151.

was enforced through divine sanction.[30] Solomon, therefore, had the leverage to use his subjects for his personal ambitions. However, in the particular case of Solomon and his son Rehoboam, we are not only faced with the general loss of freedom by the vast majority of the people and the limitations placed on them in terms of taxation and military or labor conscription, but the policy of singling out a particular section of the state as a target for harsh treatment. Although Solomon reigned over Israel and Judah, his actions alienated the northern tribes. It is from this background of alienation and discrimination that the northerners (all Israel), with the backing of Jeroboam, met Rehoboam at Shechem to decide his fate as their king.

It is important to note the character Jeroboam in the midst of this development. As indicated earlier, he was one of Solomon's officials, but fell out of favor (cf. 1 Kgs 11:26–40). The reason as indicated in the narrative was because he lifted his hands against the king for certain building projects Solomon carried out (vv. 26–27). As the narrative stands, it is difficult to make sense of the exact nature of the rivalry between Solomon and Jeroboam, although v. 40 suggests that the motivation for Jeroboam's revolt was Ahijah's prophecy (vv. 31–39). Whatever the case might be, it is well within possibility to posit that Jeroboam was involved in some form of public incitement. Thus Rabbinic exegesis explained Jeroboam's rebellious act as inciting the public against Solomon.[31] As an insider to Solomon's administration and policies, Jeroboam had enough information to incite trouble. Accordingly, the importance of his figure, which becomes evident as the story unfolds, was due to the leadership qualities he exuded and the hope he instilled in the Israelites. Besides, as Solomon was drawn to him because of his physique and abilities (the narrator describes Jeroboam as able and hard working, see v. 28), so would "all Israel" find inspiration in his personality.

---

30. Knight, "Political Rights," 100–101.
31. Cogan, *1 Kings*, 338.

## Reading 1 Kings 12:1–20

### "All Israel"[32] Meet Rehoboam (1 Kings 12:1–4)

Freire explains that intensive reflection on oneself in relation to society, that is *conscientization,* is a necessary precursor to engaging in social or political change.[33] Similarly, Gutierrez suggests that fundamental change in a person's consciousness is a necessary impetus for engaging in empowering social action: one has to perceive oneself as a subject and not an object in order to be capable of changing the social order.[34] This initial stage of the empowerment process could be through an external factor or an internal reflection on one's relationship to the environment. Irrespective of its source, *conscientization* assumes that humans have an inherent power to initiate a positive change. This inherent human potential for change was manifested during "all Israel's" encounter with Rehoboam. After being made king in Judah, Rehoboam journeyed to Shechem. He went to Shechem because "all Israel" had gathered there to make him king. The first empowering step by "all Israel" was the choice of Shechem as the place of meeting.[35] According to Walton, Matthews, and Chavalas, the choice of Shechem for this political summit meeting suggests two things. First, Rehoboam was in a weak political situation in comparison to David.[36] Second, Rehoboam demonstrated a "lack of insight and administrative finesse."[37] On the other hand, this choice, when perceived from the perspective

---

32. The term "all Israel" refers not to the larger unity David forced between the tribes, but to the northern tribes alone. See Anderson, *Living Word of the Old Testament*, 234; McEntire, *Blood of Abel*, 93.
33. See Morrow and Torres, *Reading Freire and Habermas*, 103.
34. Gutierrez, "Understanding the Empowerment Process," 230.
35. Shechem was an important town, rich in historical associations (cf. Judges 9 and Joshua 24). When anything important was to happen the Israelites gathered there.
36. It will be recalled that the elders of Israel went to David in Hebron to negotiate with him separately (2 Sam 5:1–3).
37. Walton et al., *Bible Background Commentary—Old Testament*, 432.

of "all Israel," suggests not only a clever move by them, but a belief in their bargaining power.

This becomes evident in the second empowering step by "all Israel": their conviction that they had the power to choose their king. That "all Israel" gathered at Shechem to make Rehoboam king is aptly captured in the result clause of the opening statement; "for all Israel came to Shechem to make him king" (v. 1b).[38] The Hebrew expression "to make him king" (*lehamlik 'oto*) is central to the entire narrative. As a verb phrase in the hiphil, *lehamlik* has "all Israel" as its subject.[39] It is they who can cause the necessary change in Rehoboam's status. Accordingly, Rehoboam is an object: he has not the power himself to be king.

The "position" of the Israelites during the reign of Solomon was that of powerlessness; however, in their encounter with Rehoboam they are the ones to make him king. Here "all Israel" are not only conscious of their "position," but also of their ability to change their fate. Two factors account for this. The first clue is provided in vv. 2–3, with the mention of Jeroboam. Although these verses have been a subject of much debate, what is important is the placement of Jeroboam in the context of the people's negotiation with Rehoboam.[40] He is connected in one way or the other to the actions of "all Israel." Within the two verses, his name appears three times; and he assumes both an active and a passive role in the verses (he heard, and he was sent for, and he led "all Israel" to speak to Solomon). If these pieces of informa-

---

38. All translations are mine. I have tried to give a literal translation as much as possible.

39. The hiphil is a Hebrew verbal stem that expresses a causative type of action with an active voice.

40. Vv. 2–3 and v. 12 are difficult to understand in the MT text. As they stand, they contradict v. 20. I have resolved the tension by placing Jeroboam in Egypt during the confrontation between "all Israel" and Rehoboam, and it was after "all Israel" rebelled against Solomon, then they summoned him. Thus he was not directly involved in the negotiations with Rehoboam. Nonetheless, the attempt by the narrator to place him in the midst of the negotiations signals Jeroboam's interest and influence in the encounter between "all Israel" and Rehoboam.

tion are tied to 1 Kgs 11:26–40, we cannot help but see Jeroboam as an external factor, whether overt or covert, for the change we see in "all Israel."

Although the narrator is silent on the mental processes of "all Israel," implicitly we see a positive use of psychological asset, which accounts for the second factor of change. Psychological asset is the capacity for a group to envision. In other words, it is the ability of an individual or a group to identify an urgent need for change in their current state of living.[41] Such a step represents a consciousness of themselves, because they begin to identify the problems in their present situation and devise ways to curb them. Through this, people get to know who they are and what they are capable of. The significance of this self realization is that individuals or groups are their own agents for positive change. For the Israelites, the first time they speak demonstrates an acknowledgement of their psychological asset. They tell Rehoboam, "Your father hardened our yoke, but now you make light the hard service of your father and his heavy yoke he put on us and we will serve you" (v. 4).

This is an intriguing statement, one that can only come from a people who are not afraid to seek their wellbeing. It also demonstrates clever negotiation skills from the people. It begins with the phrase "your father" (*'avika*), then continues with the unfair treatment of Solomon. Following immediately is a request and ending the statement is a proposal.

By beginning with "your father" (*'avika*) and repeating the phrase again in the same line, "all Israel" point out that Solomon is mainly responsible for their misery, and not Rehoboam. While Solomon made "heavy their yoke" (*hiqshah e't-'ullenu*), Rehoboam is to "make light" (*haqel*) the hard service Solomon placed on them (*natan 'alenu*). Father and son are juxtaposed to illustrate what happened in the past and what is to happen in the present or immediate future. But the present or immediate future carries more importance to the people than the past. This is discernible from the second part of the verse. The pronoun "you" (*'atah*), in the verbal clause, places more emphasis on Reho-

---

41. Alsop et al., *Empowerment in Practice*, 11–12.

boam.[42] He is the key to their desired state. This concern for the future is heightened by the independent adverb "now" (*'atah*).[43] The adverb serves as a logical connection to what precedes it. Therefore, although Solomon caused their hardship, now is the time for Rehoboam to change that.

While "all Israel" are more concerned with the actions of Rehoboam in the present or immediate future, one sees the conscious effort on their part to also make Solomon their "devil." In their rhetoric, the argument that Rehoboam is not Solomon stands very tall. Solomon is the subject responsible for their suffering while Rehoboam is the subject to lessen their suffering. By this rhetoric, they distance Rehoboam from the crimes of his father. This rhetorical strategy is meant to make Rehoboam understand that he is different from his father and therefore can make his own choices. Accordingly, he should be wise to grant them their request for leniency. Despite this strategic move by "all Israel," they also anticipate that anything is possible: their request could be accepted or rejected. Therefore, they make their request a conditional one. They will serve Rehoboam only when he reduces the yoke Solomon placed heavily on them. If power is the ability to make one do something one would not have done, then, "all Israel," by this condition, try to reverse, though temporarily, the balance of power in order to change their fate. Thus through their encounter with Rehoboam, "all Israel" demonstrate that they indeed wield some form of power to determine the all-important decision of who rules them. For "all Israel," such a person should be prepared to take their interests to heart.

So far in their encounter with Rehoboam, "all Israel" demonstrate an amazing display of confidence and a strong will to seek their own wellbeing. When people resolve to achieve a goal, they are hardly stopped by a challenge. Again, for a people to be conscious of their dignity and self-respect is for them to be

---

42. Gibson, *Davidson's Grammar*, 2.
43. The similarity in the transliteration of the Hebrew words "you" and "now" is because I have chosen to use the ordinary style for transliteration as prescribed by Alexander, *SBL Handbook of Style*, 28. The words are spelled differently in Hebrew.

armed. Their armor of dignity and self-respect is predicated on the premise that they are equally knowledgeable about what is good for them. By this, they put into perspective the principle of the bottom-up decision making process, which is central to the concept of participation.[44] In other words, they do not want the king (Rehoboam) and his close associates deciding for them as was done during Solomon's era. In this particular case, they (from the bottom) want to be active participants in policies that bear directly on their lives.

As a king in Judah, Rehoboam meets "all Israel" with his kingly entourage including some form of security (cf. 1 Kgs 12:18). This status of Rehoboam, however, does not intimidate "all Israel" in their present encounter. For "all Israel," their request is a legitimate one. There is, therefore, no need for fear or panic. After all, they do not call for an abolishment of the heavy yoke placed on them, neither do they oppose Rehoboam's rule. What they demand is humane treatment. By their legitimate request, "all Israel" demonstrate that they are not interested in fomenting trouble. They are ready to work, but their working conditions should uphold their dignity as humans. Though they are not there to foment trouble, they do not mince words in pointing out Solomon's harsh measures. Two words, "make hard" (*qasah*) and "heavy" (*kaved*), are used to depict the nature of the servitude Solomon placed on them. Their language is reminiscent of the slavery that the Israelites suffered in Egypt (cf. Exod 1:11–14). By putting their request forward to Rehoboam, "all Israel" exhibit their desire to participate in decisions concerning their lives. As humans who reason, they should contribute to the nature of their work. Here the actions of "all Israel" resonate with numerous labor groups all over the world that have emerged as a response to unbridled greed within the world economic system. The need to participate becomes imperative, especially when it is evident that conscious effort is made by the leadership to denigrate a section of the society for their personal gain.

---

44. See Lovan et al., *Participatory Governance*.

However, for a group to successfully react to oppression in order to effect a positive change it is not by a merely spontaneous move. Rather, such a challenging step demands deep thinking aimed at exploring what one has and how it can be put into positive use. This is what "all Israel" did. Though subordinates in their encounter with Rehoboam, "all Israel" were resolved to change their situation. Solomon's death provided them the opportunity to do just that. Solomon did not enter into an agreement with Israel to rule them, but his son Rehoboam, like his grandfather, David, needed the consent of the Israelites in order to be their king (cf. 2 Sam 5:1–3). This consent became an asset belonging to "all Israel." All they had to do was to put it into use: hence the condition attached to their request to Rehoboam. To be empowered is to have a sense of dignity, to make decisions and be responsible for them. We see these positive steps in "all Israel." For the Israelites to register their displeasure is a clear case of self-respect. To bargain with Rehoboam was an important decision they took; one in which they were prepared to face the consequences.

### *Rehoboam Consults His Advisors (1 Kings 12:6–11)*

When the narrative began, Rehoboam journeyed to Shechem to be made king. By the close of the first scene, Rehoboam had his fate hanging in the balance because the people put forward a brave request tied to a condition. Evidently, Rehoboam was dealing with a very clever people. He sensed this and retarded his response. He told them to depart and return for his answer in three days time (v. 5). "All Israel" had succeeded in delaying such an important step in the life of Rehoboam. He needed to think about the request of the people and solicit various views. The consultative process he intended to embark on would give him the opportunity to listen to different views from different people. Polzin writes that "seeking royal counsel involved weighing the recommendations of one advisor against those of another."⁴⁵ This course of action is in line with the principles of participation. After all, one person cannot profess to know all.

In vv. 6–15 we see how Rehoboam embarked on his consultative process and how he eventually answered the people who held the key to his kingship. The narrator draws our attention to this process through the use of the words "to counsel" (*ya'ats*) and "advice" (*'etsa'*). The word *ya'ats* appears six times, twice in v. 6, twice in v. 8, once in v. 9 and v. 13. As a verb, *ya'ats* depicts Rehoboam's quest for counsel in order to have an answer for the people. In four appearances of *ya'ats*, Rehoboam is the object of the verb while he is the subject in the other two. Accordingly, he consults (*ya'ats*) and asks to be counselled (*ya'ats*) in order to get the right answer for the people (cf. v. 6, v. 8, and v. 9).

The word *'etsa'* on the other hand appears three times and is used as a noun (v. 8, v. 13, and v. 14). In all its three appearances, *'etsa'* is a *nomen regens* of a construct formation. It has the phrases "the elders" (*hazzeqenim*) and "the youth" (*hayladim*) as its genitive (cf. v. 8, v. 13, and v. 14). These words put into perspective the sources of the advice Rehoboam seeks. In v. 8 and v. 13 *'etsa'* appears in the narrator's evaluative clause "he forsook the counsel of the elders." The narrator, by this repetition, emphasizes Rehoboam's rejection of the counsel he took from the elders. In v. 14, *'etsa'* appears in the clause "and he spoke to them according to the counsel of the youth." In this case, the narrator points out Rehoboam's acceptance of the counsel of the youth.

Verse 8 serves as a turning point in this scene. First, a narrative summary begins the verse: "and he forsook the counsel of the elders." Second, we see a concentration of the words *ya'ats* and *'etsa'* in the verse. The narrative summary follows immediately after the elders give their counsel (v. 7) and precedes Rehoboam's consultation with the youth. What happens then is that after listening to the elders speak, Rehoboam immediately ignores their counsel and goes to consult (*ya'ats*) the youth. By this, the narrator depicts the hastiness in Reho-

---

45. Polzin, *David and the Deuteronomist*, 178.

boam's character. No moment of thought is assigned to what the elders said. It is rejected outright, almost immediately it is uttered. Again, there is the implicit juxtaposition of the elders and the youth: which will Rehoboam eventually align with?[46] The narrator does not hold this suspense for long. Half way through v. 8, we already know that Rehoboam will opt for the counsel the youth will provide. All this is to reveal Rehoboam as an unwise leader, one who does not listen to all sides before making his final decision. Indeed the way he refers to "all Israel" as "this people" (v. 6 and v. 9), when he consults the elders and the youth, reveals his detachment from the Israelites. While "all Israel" see Rehoboam as their potential king, what Rehoboam sees in "all Israel" is "this people." Rehoboam's refusal to use a word or phrase that draws a connection between him and the Israelites shows his detachment from "all Israel." Lasine therefore writes: "Rehoboam is portrayed as imitating Solomon's desires, explicitly outdoing his father in tyrannical traits such as taxation, forced labor and coercion, the very traits that are muted in the Solomon narrative itself."[47] His consultative process, which initially is commendable, is now flawed by his hastiness and lack of insight as well as his lack of respect for the people.

## *"All Israel's" Response to Rehoboam (1 Kings 12:12–20)*

Three days pass and the people return for their answer from Rehoboam.[48] Rehoboam follows the counsel of the youth by repeating verbatim what they told him. He only decides to leave

---

46. Organ, "The Man Who Would Be King," 127, believes the terms *hazzeqenim* and *hayladim* are a stereotypical way of labeling the "elders" as wise and the "youth" as fools. Walsh, *1 Kings*, 162, also argues that the term *hazzeqenim* may "connote the wisdom that comes with age and experience" and in this context "it probably means both, since those people belong to the previous generation of royal advisors." The term *hayladim* however refers to those who were taken into service by Rehoboam and had no experience.

47. Lasine, *Knowing Kings*, 159.

48. Here again we meet Jeroboam; and although the narrator makes him explicit, he is the invisible hand that pushes "all Israel" on, giving them support in their quest for fair treatment.

out the clause "my little finger is thicker than the loins of my father" (v. 14). This omission could be because of its derogatory tone and the bad image he would create of his father. Surprisingly, Rehoboam seems more careful about degrading his father's image in public than lessening the plight of the Israelites. In v. 15 we are informed that Rehoboam did not "hearken" (*shama'*) to the people. This information is repeated again in the opening of v. 16. In v. 15, the information is given by the narrator as a background to the theological explanation of the turn of events. That is, Rehoboam fails to listen (*shama'*) to the people because Yahweh has intended this to happen.[49] In v. 16, however, it is the people who realize that Rehoboam has not hearkened (*shama'*) to them. The importance of the word in this scene calls for more attention.

*Shama'*, mostly translated "to hear," has a wide usage in the Hebrew Bible, with a nuanced meaning in many contexts. As part of the Israelite call to worship (the *Shema*) and used extensively by the prophets (cf. Amos 4:1; Isa 6:4–5; Ezek 18:25), *shama'* "embraces the ideas of understanding and obeying."[50] The act of hearkening/hearing emerges as an integral aspect of Israelite society and as Crenshaw points out, "the hearing heart" in ancient Israel is so crucial that it assumes the same status as a sage in ancient Egypt.[51] Rehoboam's failure to "hearken" to the people means he fails to share in the people's plight. He lacks the ability to discern the genuine concerns of the people and their desire to be heard. He, accordingly, emerges as a fool.[52]

Again, that Rehoboam failed to "hearken" (*shama'*) to the people accentuates the poor relationship between him and the people. The first meeting between the two sides was held in an optimistic atmosphere. Rehoboam listened to the people and told

---

49. According to von Rad, *Problem of the Hexatuech*, 208, "Through the use of this prophecy/fulfillment schema, the Deuteronomist reaffirms the legitimacy of Jeroboam's ascent to power."

50. Carpenter and Comfort, *Holman Treasury*, vii.

51. Crenshaw, *Old Testament Wisdom*, 33.

52. The characterization of Rehoboam as a fool is strengthened by his alignment with the "youth," which, as Organ points out, falls in line with the character of the "fool" in wisdom literature.

them to depart for an answer in three days time. "All Israel" on their part did not react negatively; they did not insist on an answer there and then. After Rehoboam embarked on his consultative process, however, the optimism gave way to suspicion and disregard on his part towards the people. For Rehoboam not to "hearken" to the people, therefore, signifies his total disregard for "all Israel," the very people who were to make him king.

His failure to "hearken" (*shama'*) to the people led the people to "return" (*shuv*) a word to him (v. 16). Ironically, when Rehoboam consulted his advisors, he was looking for a way to "return" (*shuv*) a word to the people. His "returned words" led to dissatisfaction and then he was the recipient of a "returned word" from the people. Interestingly, the ditty of the people to Rehoboam resurrected an old rebellion cry that put into sharp focus the deep hidden divisions between the northern tribes and Judah. By invoking the old rebellion cry against the house of David, "all Israel" made it clear that they severed the relationship between Judah and the northern tribes (Israel).

Rehoboam realised his loss and attempted to use force by sending Adoram (whom the narrator describes as being in charge of the forced labor) to get the people to perhaps submit to him.[53] "All Israel" replied by stoning Adoram to death. By this brave act, they unambiguously warned Rehoboam of their preparedness to assert themselves if need be in order to drum home their message that they no longer owed allegiance to him. The use of force by "all Israel" was, therefore, reactive and defensive. Force was an option for them because its absence would jeopardize their achievements so far.

The rejection of Rehoboam opened up the way for a new leader for the Israelites. We are not surprised to see Jeroboam as this new leader. Indeed, v. 20 affirms the view that the narrative of 1 Kings 1–20, although explaining the role of Rehoboam in the division, as well as highlighting the part played by the people, also intends to narrate the rise of Jeroboam in fulfillment

---

53. I believe the narrator intended to indicate that Rehoboam tried using force when the narrator explicated further that Adoram was in charge of the forced labor.

of Ahijah's prophecy.[54] In many respects, Jeroboam had been the shadow leader of the northerners. His return from his self-imposed exile in Egypt, especially at the moment when relations between Rehoboam and "all Israel" had turned very sour, at the very least hints at his personal interest and involvement in the whole saga. It is important to note, nonetheless, that "all Israel" still held the power to choose their leader. The structure of the verse places Jeroboam just like Rehoboam in the object position. This closure to the narrative echoes the all-important issue of reserving the power to choose leaders for the people, irrespective of the role individual figures might have played in advancing the rights of the people.

## *Conclusion*

Empowerment is a modern concept used in development discourse to reveal the inherent potential of humans to seek their wellbeing. Development agents and groups promote these concepts with the conviction that when people are empowered and demand participation they change their societies for the better. Reading the text from the perspective of this concept has revealed, though in a rudimentary manner, the concerns of such sentiments in ancient times. More importantly, we have come to realize that "all Israel" were not passive in the split of the united monarchy. On the contrary, they were active participants in the turn of events. When the narrative began, "all Israel" met Rehoboam at Shechem to make him king. At the close of it, "all Israel" instead made Jeroboam king. The introduction and conclusion highlight "all Israel's" power of refusing to make Rehoboam king on the one hand and causing Jeroboam to be king on the other hand. As empowered people, "all Israel" demanded the right to participate in decisions that bore on their lives. Throughout the narrative, their desire to end the inhumane treatment meted out to them drove them to take calculated steps to ensure their freedom from a potentially tyrannical rule by Rehoboam.

---

54. Long, *1 Kings*, 137.

However, while we acknowledge the role of "all Israel," Jeroboam's role also needs to be recognized, since he, in many ways, served as a stimulus for their brave act. Jeroboam was a source of hope and strength for the Israelites. As an industrious and successful young man, Jeroboam was promoted by Solomon to a high position of responsibility. In a clandestine encounter with a shadowy prophet, Jeroboam was proclaimed a legitimate successor of the king due to widespread corrosion of faithfulness. Political incompetence and divine intervention paved the way for him to be chosen by his people as their leader.

This portrait finds expression in many African societies, especially during their struggles for freedom. The leadership role of Mandela in South Africa and Kwame Nkrumah in Ghana are just two examples. Interestingly, Jeroboam, the favored of Yahweh, ironically descended the same path as Solomon, and even became the archetypal sinner and the standard for judging the subsequent leaders of Israel.[55] This portrait also resonates with several African examples where promising leaders turned out to be despots. For instance, Zimbabwe's Robert Mugabe and the late Muammar al Gaddafi of Libya were once celebrated icons of the struggle against oppression and dictatorship. After establishing their hold on power, they presided over some of the most repressive regimes on the continent.

The narrative of 1 Kgs 12:1–20 is pivotal in Israel's royal history. Here Israel's political landscape changed, never to return to its former state. What this paper has sought to do is to explain the role played by "all Israel," with the backing of the young and promising Jeroboam, in charting this new course. Acknowledging the contribution of "all Israel" is a step in the right direction, a step that resonates with the situations of our own times.

---

55. Ibid., 132, Long points out the continuity between the materials on Solomon and Jeroboam. Here, there is an irony in the character of Jeroboam. Emerging as the choice of Yahweh to punish the house of David, he later develops into the archetypal sinner of Israel.

*Bibliography*

Alexander, Patrick H. et al., eds. *SBL Handbook of Style*. Peabody, MA: Hendrickson, 1999.

Alsop, Ruth, Mette F. Bertelsen, and Jeremy Holland. *Empowerment in Practice: From Analysis to Implementation*. Washington, DC: World Bank, 2006.

Anderson, Bernhard W. *The Living Word of the Old Testament*. 3rd ed. London: Longman, 1978.

Carpenter, Eugene E., and Philip W. Comfort. *Holman Treasury of Key Bible Words: 200 Greek and 200 Hebrew Words Explained and Defined*. Nashville: Broadman & Holman, 2000.

Carr, E. Summerson. "Rethinking Empowerment Theory Using a Feminist Lens: The Importance of Process." *Affilia* 18 no.1 (2003) 8–20.

Cogan, M. *1 Kings: A New Translation with Introduction and Commentary*. New Haven, CT: Yale University Press, 2008.

Crenshaw, James L. *Old Testament Wisdom: An Introduction*. Atlanta: John Knox, 1981.

Cross, Frank M. *Canaanite Myth and Hebrew Epic: Essays in the History of the Religion of Israel*. Cambridge, MA: Harvard University Press, 1973.

Devries, Simon J. *1 Kings*. WBC 12. Waco, TX: Word, 1985.

Donner, Herbert. "The Separate States of Israel and Judah." In *Israelite and Judean History*, edited by John H. Hayes and J. Maxwell Miller, 381–434. London: SCM, 1977.

Finkelstein, Israel, and Neil A. Silberman. *The Bible Unearthed*. New York: Free Press, 2001.

Gibson, J. C. L. *Davidson's Introductory Hebrew Grammar—Syntax*. 4th ed. Edinburgh: T. & T. Clark, 1994.

Gutierrez, Lorraine M. "Understanding the Empowerment Process: Does Consciousness Make a Difference?" *Social Work Research* 19 (1995) 229–37.

Gyekye, Kwame. *African Cultural Values: An Introduction*. Accra: Sankofa, 1996.

Halpern, Baruch. "Sectionalism and the Schism." *JBL* 93 (1974) 519–32.

Hayes, A. D. H. "The Period of the Judges and the Rise of the Monarchy." In *Israelite and Judaean History*, edited by John H. Hayes and J. Maxwell Miller, 285–331. London: SCM, 1977.

Hayes, John H. *Introduction to the Bible*. Philadelphia: Westminster, 1971.

Knight, Douglas A. "Political Rights and Powers in Monarchic Israel." *Semia* 66 (1994) 93–117.

Lasine, Stuart. *Knowing Kings—Knowledge, Power and Narcissism in the Hebrew Bible*. Atlanta: SBL, 2001.

Long, Burke O. *1 Kings, with an Introduction to Historical Literature*. Grand Rapids: Eerdmans, 1984.

Lovan, W. Robert, Michael Murray, and Ron Raffer. *Participatory Governance: Planning, Conflict Mediation and Public Decision Making in Civil Society*. Aldershot, Burlington, ON: Ashgate, 2004.

McEntire, Mark H. *The Blood of Abel: The Violent Plot in the Hebrew Bible*. Macon, GA: Mercer University Press, 1999.

Morrow, Raymond Allen, and Carlos Alberto Torres. *Reading Freire and Habermas: Critical Pedagogy and Transformative Social Change*. New York: Teachers College Press, 2002.

Narayan-Parkeer, Deepa. *Empowerment and Poverty Reduction: A Source Book*. Washington, DC: World Bank, 2002.

Organ, Barbra E. "'The Man Who Would Be King': Irony in the Story of Rehoboam." In *From Babel to Babylon: Essays on Biblical History and Literature in Honour of Brian Peckham*, edited by Joyce Rilett Wood, John E. Harvey, and Mark Leuchter, 124–32. New York: T. & T. Clark, 2006.

Petesch, Patti, Catalina Smulovitz, and Michael Walton. "Evaluating Empowerment: A Framework with Cases from Latin America." In *Measuring Empowerment: Cross Disciplinary Perspectives*, edited by Deepa Narayan-Parker, 39–68. Washington, DC: World Bank, 2005.

Pollack, Kenneth M. "Introduction: Understanding the Arab Awakening." In *The Arab Awakening: America and the Transformation of the Middle East*, by Kenneth M. Pollack et al., 1–12. Washington, DC: Brookings Institution, 2011.

Polzin, Robert. *David and the Deuteronomist: A Literary Study of the Deuteronomistic History Part Three, 2 Samuel*. Indianapolis: Indiana University Press, 1993.

Rappaport, Julian. "Studies in Empowerment: Introduction to the Issue." In *Studies in Empowerment: Steps toward Understanding and Action*, edited by J. Rappaport, C. Swift, and R. Hess, 1–8. New York: Hayworth, 1984.

Sadan, Elisheva. *Empowerment and Community Planning: Theory and Practice of People-Focused Social Solutions*.

Translated by Richard Flantz. Tel Aviv: Hakibbutz Hameuchad, 1997.

Soggin, J. Alberto. "The Davidic-Solomonic Kingdom." In *Israelite and Judean History*, edited by John H. Hayes and J. Maxwell Miller, 332–80. London: SCM, 1977.

Sweeney, Marvin A. "The Critique of Solomon in the Josianic Editions of the Deuteronomistic History." *JBL* 114 (1995) 607–22.

Walsh, Jerome T. *1 Kings: Berit Olam Studies in Hebrew Narrative and Poetry*. Collegeville, MN: Liturgical, 1996.

———. *Old Testament Narrative: A Guide to Interpretation*. Louisville: Westminster John Knox, 2009.

Walton, J. H., V. H. Matthews, and M. W. Chavalas. *The IVP Bible Background Commentary—Old Testament*. Downers Grove, IL: InterVarsity, 2000.

von Rad, Gerhard. *The Problem of the Hexatuech and Other Essays*. New York: McGraw-Hill, 1966.

Zimmerman, Marc A. "Taking Aim on Empowerment Research: On the Distinction between Individual and Psychological Conceptions." *American Journal of Community Psychology* 18.1 (1990) 169–77.

# An Overview and Analysis of the Present Discussion between Theology and Music

Bradley K. Broadhead
McMaster Divinity College, Hamilton, ON, Canada

## Introduction

Only six years after Jeremy S. Begbie's lament that "[m]usic has received virtually no sustained treatment in contemporary systematic theology,"[1] Philip E. Stoltzfus could say, "Since the close of the twentieth century, there has emerged a sudden flowering of theological commentary on music and musical aesthetics."[2] It appears that a new interdisciplinary field is emerging at the point of the intersection between theology and music. This is not to overlook historical writings on the significance of music to religious practice,[3] or to say that there was a complete absence of theological reflection on music prior to the twenty-first century, but rather to note that there has been a recent trend towards a direct and focused engagement between theology and music. It is my intent to examine and assess this trend to see what these engagements share in common and to suggest ways in which the discussion can be moved forward.

I will limit the scope of my inquiry by setting up three criteria to determine whether a given work will be considered: First, the work in question must reflect a sustained engagement between music and theology; it must go beyond brief allusions to music for illustrative purposes. Second, the work must engage with music itself and/or its means of production and reception. The

---

1. Begbie, *Theology, Music and Time*, 3.
2. Stoltzfus, *Theology as Performance*, 12.
3. See Stapert, *A New Song*, for an overview of how the early church thought of music.

latter may include the circumstances out of which the music emerges insofar as it is demonstrably relevant to the production of this music. In other words, the focus must be on the qualities and characteristics of music as opposed to the words and/or images and personalities it may happen to accompany. Third, the theological framework interacting with music must be at least broadly Christian.[4]

Even through the lens of this narrowed scope, the field of theology and music is filled with many different, and often competing, agendas. This may be due in part to the fact that musical notes and phrases by themselves, unlike words and sentences, do not make reference to phenomena outside of themselves, although they easily *associate* with extrinsic elements. This penchant for association allows music to be utilized by a spectrum of views diverse enough to encompass everything from a conservative orthodoxy to process theology and feminism.

In order to discern what trends are emerging in the midst of this diversity, it is necessary to create some methodological categories. For Begbie, the intersection of theology and music involves two basic approaches: the first being the "bearing of theology on the arts"[5] (including music) and the second being "the ways in which music can benefit theology."[6] Begbie acknowledges that these two are interrelated, but his own works show a marked difference in relation to his approach.[7] While helpful, these categories are too narrow in terms of Begbie's use of them, or too broad when expanded theoretically for the current task. Alternatively, Stoltzfus suggests arranging the field around the projects of prominent authors: "One can observe in the new literature three theological-aesthetic options taking shape: Albert Blackwell's "sacred in music," Heidi Epstein's "feminist

---

4. The intersection of theology and music may be of interest to the broader study of religion and to other faiths as well. At present, however, most writers are operating with a broadly Christian framework.
5. Begbie, *Voicing Creation's Praise*, xviii.
6. Begbie, *Theology, Music and Time*, 5.
7. Compare Begbie, *Voicing Creation's Praise*, and Begbie, *Resounding Truth*, which take the first approach, with Begbie, *Theology, Music and Time*, where he adopts the second.

theology of music," and Jeremy Begbie's "theology through music."[8] I believe Stoltzfus is on to something here, but these categories are a little too narrow: these individuals are certainly key players in the emergence of studies on theology and music, but they have yet to inspire substantial secondary literature or followers who have furthered their approaches in significant ways. Categories are needed that have the potential to encompass not only these major players, but also the work of their lesser-known colleagues in the field, as well as previous forays into the area. Expanding Stoltzfus's categories should provide a taxonomy that is able to meet this need.[9]

I propose organising the field of theology and music according to the following methodological categories: The first is aesthetics, by which I mean beauty and transcendence in relation to God. Contra Stoltzfus, it seems to me that "the theological aesthetics of beauty"[10] remain part of emerging discussion in the field; in fact Blackwell's approach exemplifies this. Expanding the "sacred in music" to aesthetics allows me to include the insights of the likes of Richard Viladesau in *Theology and the Arts: Encountering God through Music, Art and Rhetoric*. The second is a dialogue through analogy, by which I mean drawing relevant connections between aspects of music and aspects of theology, hopefully resulting in mutually edifying insights. This category encompasses much of Begbie's approach, especially when he is exploring what music can do for theology. It also leaves room for the fascinating enterprise of Francis Young in *The Art of Performance*. The third is primarily defined by

---

8. Stoltzfus, *Theology as Performance*, 12. See Blackwell, *Sacred in Music*; Epstein, *Melting the Venusberg*; Begbie, *Theology, Music and Time*. Presumably, Stoltzfus would add to this his own category of "theology as performance."

9. Unfortunately, while I interact with Stoltzfus's useful survey of this area and expand on his categories, I lack space to deal with the bulk of his own work. Since much of it revolves around an analysis of the relationship of Schleiermacher, Barth, and Wittgenstein to music instead of focusing on music on its own terms in relation to theology, I pass over it in favor of other works more suited to my own endeavor.

10. Stoltzfus, *Theology as Performance*, 12.

Epstein's feminist deconstruction and reconstruction of the dialogue between theology and music, though reference will also be made to Ann Pederson.[11] The feminist approach stands alone until such a time as other ideological critiques and reconstructions can complement or further its project. These broad categories should suffice as a way of organizing the emerging dialogue between theology and music.

Finally, I aim to be comprehensive but not exhaustive in this undertaking. I have selected a number of significant works that fit into my expanded categories, providing me with enough space for critical interaction and assessment.

## Theology and Musical Aesthetics

Richard Viladesau observes that, "it is clear that for a long time aesthetics was located more or less at the periphery of Christian thought . . . [but] in recent years it has moved into a much more central position of theological prominence."[12] In his review essay, "Aesthetics, Music, and Theology," Frank Brown links this movement to the postmodern deconstruction of formalism and aestheticism, which he says has opened vistas to theology once closed by the perception of art "as something whose intrinsic aesthetic purposes could never be subject to moral or theological criteria, except in some secondary sort of way."[13] Several significant works around the close of the twentieth century and the beginning of the twenty-first have exploited this opening. For my purposes, I will be examining works in which musical aesthetics connect theology to music by exploring theological traits inherent in music. In other words, the dialogue between musical aesthetics and theology is based on the premise that music can tell us something about God, distinguishing it from the analogical approach to linking music and theology

---

11. Ann Pederson writes about music and theology from a feminist perspective (see Pederson, *God, Creation, and All That Jazz*, ix), but I agree with Stoltzfus that her project has more in common with Begbie's. See Stoltzfus, *Theology as Performance*, 15.
12. Viladesau, *Theological Aesthetics*, 2.
13. Brown, "Aesthetics, Music, and Theology," 32.

below, concerned as it is with finding parallels and systems of relations.

## Richard Viladesau

I begin with Viladesau, not because his work is chronologically prior to others, but rather because he is remarkably direct and succinct about his undertaking. The heart of his book, *Theology and the Arts: Encountering God through Music, Art and Rhetoric*,[14] is explicated in the book's final chapter, in which he sets out his "underlying theses": first, "God is ultimate beauty, implicitly known as the ultimate desire of the human mind and heart"; second, "[r]evelation is the self-gift of God to humanity," in which God reveals himself in events in history, culminating in the Incarnation; and third, "[a]rt is one of the primary embodiments of the ongoing history of this revelation and its communication."[15] From these theses, he concludes:

> Theology, as a reflection on revelation, should be related to art in two ways: academically, theology must reflect on beauty, on art, and on the products of the arts, as part of its object; and pastorally, the arts of ministry must incorporate theology as an intrinsic part of their functioning.[16]

For the sake of my own objectives, I will be focusing on the former part of his project, without denying the value of the latter. Since the present discussion concerns music and theology as opposed to aesthetics in general, I will focus my overview and analysis on the first chapter, where he employs music to illustrate the theme of his work: "artistic beauty as a means of the mind's 'ascent' to God—or, from another point of view, as a medium of divine self-revelation."[17] In Viladesau's schema, music is joined to theology by taking up the object of theology;

---

14. Viladesau's earlier work engages with aesthetics in a broad sense, but does not deal with music in a direct and sustained manner. See Viladesau, *Theological Aesthetics*.
15. Viladesau, *Theology and the Arts*, 218.
16. Ibid.
17. Ibid., 4.

because God "is ultimate beauty," finding beauty in music points the listener towards God's ultimate beauty.

The chapter in question begins with a survey of the historical relationship between music and Christianity, noting that it was marked by ambivalence, suggesting that the reasons for this lie in "(1) the pagan associations of music in the ancient world; (2) the conflict between spirituality and immersion in the sense experience; (3) a certain competition between musical art and the word."[18] Viladesau then endeavors to answer these problems in inverse order. He first acknowledges the primacy of the word in Scripture, but suggests via Aquinas and Luther that, in terms of liturgy, this need not be an either/or decision and goes on to ask whether there might in fact be "a legitimate and valid approach to God through music and art."[19] Second, he works from the premise that music engages "the heart by representing emotional states, and [engages] the mind by evoking the meanings associated with those states in the human mind," to argue that music as a sense experience in fact leads to a spiritual awakening via beauty to the contemplation of God.[20] Finally, Viladesau contextualizes the link between music and ancient paganism by bringing up the question of liturgy, acknowledging the potential of music to distract from worship, but also pointing out its value in underlining incarnational theology and concludes with a call to use music with prudence and discretion.

Viladesau's engagement with music in the wider dialogue between aesthetics and theology provides a well-reasoned foundation for further exploration and discovery. It is noteworthy that as a Roman Catholic he also draws upon the Protestant tradition, broadening the appeal and the basis for his enterprise.[21]

---

18. Ibid., 28.
19. Ibid., 34.
20. Ibid., 38–39, 46.
21. A reviewer has noted Viladesau's sometimes misleading statements about the Eastern Orthodox tradition (it is primarily seen through the fictional work, *Doctor Zhivago*), but nonetheless warmly commends the book. See Bychkov, "Review of *Theology and the Arts*," 518.

## Albert L. Blackwell

*The Sacred in Music* appeared the same year as Viladesau's work on music and aesthetics and one year prior to Begbie's analogical venture in *Theology, Music and Time*. It represents the most thorough treatment to date connecting musical aesthetics with theology. Blackwell rests his enterprise on the premise that there is "sacramental potential" in music. His thesis is:

> that the phenomenon of music, in all its great variety, is potentially sacramental, and not only in explicitly religious contexts. Dwelling at music's heart is a sacramental potency, awaiting only appropriate times and places for its actualisation, for manifesting the holy and for expressing our experiences of the holy.[22]

He justifies using the term "sacramental" on the basis of the "flexible and commodious" use of the term *sacramentum* in the first three centuries of the Christian church and quotes Paul Tillich, Philip Sherrard, and Richard McBrien who argue for an expanded understanding of the term.[23] Finally, he comes forward with his personal conviction "that music offers divine epiphany, real presence."[24] By calling music potentially sacramental, offering a *"finite reality through which the divine is perceived to be disclosed or communicated,"*[25] Blackwell displays similarities to Viladesau's project, but goes beyond it in terms of what he claims for music.

Having made his case for his view of music, Blackwell links theology and music together in two "sacramental traditions": first, the Pythagorean tradition, that is, the contemplation of "invisible objects of our understanding and subjects of our insight," especially math and music, and second, the Incarnational tradition, that is, bodily perception, the world of matter, "objects of our senses and subjects of our desire," especially the sounds of

---

22. Blackwell, *Sacred in Music*, 28.
23. Ibid., 26–28.
24. Ibid., 29.
25. McBrien, *Catholicism*, 788. Quoted in Blackwell, *Sacred in Music*, 28, as the definition Blackwell wishes to apply to music. Italics in original and quotation.

music.[26] Balancing these traditions that emphasize body and spirit is essential to his schema. Next Blackwell moves to the relation of music to creation, beginning with Pythagorean intervals, moving through the overtone series, considering various scales and modes, the cycle of fifths, and basic chord progressions. He is not content with the European system, but also considers Asian systems and even the discovery of some ancient bells in China to support his case that "we may speak of music as a universal language in countless cultural dialects."[27] He uses this aspect of music, combined with the transcendental nature of mathematics, to contest Richard Rorty's anti-foundationalism, arguing for a world with an "intrinsic nature." This intrinsic nature, found in the Pythagorean tradition, is a revelation of its artist. Blackwell shifts to the Incarnational tradition to explore the transcendental/sacramental effects of the sound of music. After linking music and emotion with the biblical tradition, he sets to work combating the deconstruction of the transcendental in postmodern critiques of Mozart by appealing to the "immediate experience" of the appreciative listener and the ineffable expressiveness of his music, rallying luminaries such as Ludwig Wittgenstein to his aid. From these heights, Blackwell turns his attention to the Fall, considering the dissonance, tension, and chaos found in music that expresses the fallen nature of creation. The "Pythagorean Comma" describes the fact that if the cycle of fifths followed a strictly Pythagorean ratio, the cycle would not finish perfectly and thus spin indefinitely into other cycles. Blackwell concludes:

> The Pythagorean Comma, then, is like an emblem of our world, where imperfection is unavoidable. But though the Pythagorean Comma and human sinfulness are unavoidable, neither is irredeemable.... The Pythagorean Comma is redeemable through the musical process of tempering. Human sinfulness is redeemable through the religious process of salvation.[28]

---

26. Blackwell, *Sacred in Music*, 47.
27. Ibid., 72.
28. Ibid., 158.

Salvation, defined as "healing leading to wholeness, both individual and communal,"[29] is linked to the sacramental nature of music. While acknowledging that music not only has the power to heal but to harm, Blackwell focuses on music as a means of unity in diversity, uniting while resisting the totalitarian tendencies inherent in idealist or utopian views of community. His work concludes with an examination of "final bliss," in which he looks at music's ability to bring about intimacy, fulfillment, and transcendence.

Blackwell's work is sweeping in scope and daring in its undertaking. He interacts with a diverse range of scholars and musical genres, quoting them and interacting with them at length. Much of the work is autobiographical; his voice and opinions are everywhere present. This is to the reader's benefit when dealing with a subject as ephemeral, elusive, and, in terms of taste, subjective as music is. These choices have assets and drawbacks, but given Blackwell's approach, perhaps they are the right ones.

## Assessment and Projections

Vildesau and Blackwell may indeed be gazing on vistas opened up by postmodernism, but, in linking their claims about music to Christian theology, they are also reacting against postmodernism defined as a rejection of meta-narratives. In appealing to music's beauty and transcendent qualities, they are simultaneously making subjective evaluations and appealing to intrinsic (and therefore to some degree objective/universal) properties in music as a way of connecting with God. This tension may be unavoidable.

The aesthetic approach to the intersection of theology and music is a long and storied one; it is no accident that both of the authors considered above spend time in their respective works going over the historical relationship between music and the church. Given the history of Christianity, it is almost certain that the issues they address will continue to be relevant.

---

29. Ibid., 197.

## Dialogue through Analogy

The following connection made between theology and music differs from the above in that music is not so much a mode of divine revelation as a different approach to doing theology.[30] Just as a parable can assist one to see a given situation in a new light (see, for example, Nathan's parable for David's sin in 2 Sam 12:1-15), so musical analogies have the potential to shed light on theological issues. According to Dedre Gentner:

> Analogies are partial similarities between different situations that support further inferences. Specifically, analogy is a kind of similarity in which the same system of relations holds across different objects. Analogies thus capture parallels across different situations.[31]

In the present context, a given aspect of music can assist theology insofar as it can provide a "system of relations" that also holds true for some aspect of theology. The works examined below employ this method as a means of bringing together theology and music.

### Frances Young

Before Begbie openly pondered what music could do for theology, Frances Young, in *The Art of Performance*, discerned similarities between the questions being pondered in performance practice in the Western classical tradition of music and the question, "How can we live in and worship with the Bible—how can we 'perform' the Bible—in a modern world so different from the past which produced and used it?"[32] In her prologue, she makes it clear that she is constructing an analogy and not

---

30. Though it is beyond the scope of this survey, it is worth noting that theology can also influence music. Historically, there have been one or two cases in which theology has affected music theory (see, for example, Rivera, *German Music Theory*, 122, 222, where he demonstrates how Johannes Lippius's conception of the Trinity assisted him in formulating his theory of inversion), and the way the words in sacred music have affected the musical choices of composers such as J. S. Bach has been well established (see, for example, Leaver, "Motive and Motif").
31. Gentner, "Analogy," 107.
32. Young, *Art of Performance*, 1.

attempting "a study of music in the patristic period," though she does not deny the influence of the "positive use of the musical metaphor in the Fathers."[33] Young skillfully weaves her analogy through the themes of each chapter: in "Interpretation and Authenticity," exposition of the Scripture is linked to performance practice; in "Determining the Canon," the biblical canon is linked to classic musical repertoire; "Tradition and Interpretation" speak equally, and in a similar fashion, to musical and biblical concerns; "Jewish Texts and Christian Meanings" are connected with musical devices such as theme and variation, key changes, antithesis and recapitulation; "The Question of Criteria" straddles both worlds on the theme of constraint in interpretation; in "The Bible and Doctrine," the question of music's ability to convey content is paralleled by efforts to discern and extract sound doctrine from the Bible; love songs and musical transcendence are worked into the spiritual use of the Bible in "The Bible and Spirituality"; and, finally, "Improvisation and Inspiration" links musical improvisation with the limitless applications of the Scriptures. Music acts as a foil for Young's interpretive concerns; undeniably, music is serving theology, and doing the job admirably well.

Begbie acknowledges Young's work in a footnote in *Theology, Music and Time*, calling it "an illuminating essay" but placing it in the realm of biblical interpretation as opposed to theology.[34] Yet Young's work has theological implications; she does not just speak of merely understanding the Bible, but also of living and performing it. Admittedly, music is clearly the junior partner in the dialogue that she sets up, but it is a partner nonetheless. Furthermore, as seen below, Begbie himself engages in biblical interpretation when he employs a musical analogy to assist in his theological interpretation of Romans 9–11.[35] If he does not consciously borrow from her methodology, it remains evident that he, too, employs analogy in at least a

---

33. Ibid., 3.
34. Begbie, *Theology, Music and Time*, 4 n. 2.
35. Ibid., 255–70.

similar fashion in the conversation he stages between theology and music.

*Jeremy Begbie*
*Theology, Music and Time* marks a deliberate attempt to employ music in the service of theology.[36] If Young was among the first to take steps towards treating music as a full-fledged dialogue partner for theology, Begbie brought it to fruition. The book is centered on the close relationship between music and time and how this can be used to "see" challenging aspects of systematic theology in a fresh way. Begbie's serious treatment of music is evident from the first two chapters, which are devoted to an explication of the nature of music, especially with respect to time. He takes the time to situate his understanding in the context of contemporary musical thought.

When Begbie engages with theology in part two of the book, he brings an understanding of time shaped by music into dialogue with Augustine, allowing him to critique Augustine's association of temporality with fallenness. According to Begbie, temporality is an intrinsic aspect of God's creation, not to be associated with the curse. Music comes to the fore in his examination of the waves of tension and release in musical phrases as they follow each other in temporal sequence to biblical prophecy. This approach avoids many of the problems inherent in a strictly linear approach to prophecy and fulfillment, paralleling the development of musical resolutions that defer final resolution with partial fulfillments of prophecy that await their ultimate resolution in Jesus Christ. Similarly, the repetition of the Eucharist finds justification and explication when connected to "metrical music" (music played with a sense of tempo) in which repetition functions to "both close the [musical phrase] *and* provoke a

---

36. See Begbie, *Resounding Truth*, for Begbie's reversal of this approach: an engagement with music through theology. Unlike *Theology, Music and Time*, *Resounding Truth* addresses its topic through a variety of approaches in addition to analogy, including a historical look at musicians and theologians reminiscent of Stoltzfus' work. It is also much broader in scope.

desire for further fulfilment."[37] Music allows one to experience the Eucharist as a reminder of Christ's death and "a re-charging of God's promise of a new future."[38]

Part three offers musical insight gleaned from an examination of improvisation and freedom in music. The approaches of composers Pierre Boulez and John Cage are contrasted with each other; the former exerts his will over every note, tying each to a mathematical model that replaces previous groundings of music in physical reality, while the latter gives almost everything over to nature and chance. Both approaches are attempts "to be free of a supposedly oppressive teleological system (such as tonality)" but ultimately result in mathematical or temporal necessity.[39] According to Begbie, both approaches are products of a philosophy that regards "constraint as inherently detrimental to authentic freedom."[40] In contrast with these attempts to throw off constraint, he makes a case that constraint is in fact integral to freedom. The use of analogy here is not as direct as in the previous examples. Music is tied to the worldviews of those who make it, and, in this case, the musical experiments of Boulez and Cage for Begbie represent excesses to be avoided instead of emulated. The following section delves into jazz as a musical model for freedom operating with constraint. Begbie, among other things, makes analogies between the way jazz tunes develop over time and the formation of tradition in the church, and between inevitable errors made by improvisers and the "restful restlessness" of Christian freedom.[41] Finally, he connects improvising and gift-giving to the doctrine of election in Romans 9–11. God and Israel are linked in a musical improvisation during which Israel's refusal to respond to God is taken up by God and used as a means to draw the Gentiles into the church. Then, "[t]he Gentiles' improvisation will set off Jewish improvisation."[42] It is not possible to treat Begbie's nuanced treatment of

---

37. Begbie, *Theology, Music and Time*, 166.
38. Ibid., 167.
39. Ibid., 196.
40. Ibid., 197.
41. Ibid., 244.
42. Ibid., 258.

these issues fully here, but even this brief overview should serve to underline his robust use of the analogical approach.

However, his intrepid enterprise leaves something to be desired in the eyes of his contemporaries. In her own work, Epstein asserts that Begbie "reduces music to a mere proof-text for biblical doctrine."[43] It is unclear whether she is objecting to his confessional stance or if she is arguing that his theological pre-understandings are keeping him from seeing all that music has to offer. As she develops her critique, she asserts that Begbie fails to "adequately . . . ground his analysis in musical practices of particular historical contexts."[44] This is a valid concern; had Begbie addressed the social context of jazz, he would have had a resource with which to meet the concerns raised in Blackwell's review dealing with Begbie's treatment of Romans 9–11. Blackwell suggests that "Paul's Christian particularism seems out of harmony with the musical pluralism of a robust jazz ensemble."[45] Blackwell's concerns could have been pre-empted had Begbie considered the social history of race relations in jazz music, with black and white providing the analogues corresponding to Jew and Gentile. It should also be noted that, while Begbie engages directly with composers in the classical tradition, he avoids similar engagement with any major jazz figures.[46]

*Ann Pederson*
Ann Pederson stands somewhere between an analogical approach and a feminist deconstructionalist approach; in this section the former aspect will come into focus. Jazz and improvisation are the themes that dominate in *God, Creation, and All That Jazz*, and *The Music of Creation* (with Arthur Peacocke). In her first book, after situating her discussion of creation theologically, Pederson parallels classical theism with the way classical music is often performed in a contemporary context,

---

43. Epstein, *Melting the Venusberg*, 84.
44. Ibid., 87.
45. Blackwell, "Review of *Theology, Music and Time*," 474.
46. For an extended engagement with a major jazz figure from a theological perspective, see Howison, *God's Mind in That Music*.

noting the commonality of authoritarian and static interpretation. Against this, she argues that "[w]ith the advent of Einsteinian physics and evolutionary biology, the model of jazz and improvisation has come to seem more appropriate."[47] This discussion in her opening chapter on "The Composition of Creation" is followed by "creativity as creaturely vocation," where she opts for process theology as an alternative to classical theism. According to Pederson, this model gives human beings the ability to improvise as "co-creators" with God. "Perfecting the Art of Hanging Out" parallels the open and interactive dynamics of small group jazz with the wider community of creation and the Christian community in particular. In "The Blues: An Affirmation That Life Still Swings," Pederson wrestles with suffering and evil, bringing the blues into play not so much as an analogical sounding board for a theology of suffering but as a means of confronting and coping with them.[48] The concluding chapter, "The Life of the Church," is a practical chapter that combines ecclesiology very naturally with the social aspects of playing jazz and makes some practical suggestions for church practice.

In Pederson's book with scientist Arthur Peacocke, the theme of jazz and improvised music surfaces again in relation to creation. Science is also a dialogue partner in this work, but since this is not my present focus, I will highlight specifically the musical encounters pertaining to theology that it presents. One significant encounter concerns the two natures of Jesus Christ. Notes in a chord can be used as an analogy for the two natures. Both natures are present simultaneously without one having to give way to the other, just as notes in a chord sound together, so that "[t]here is no question in the Christian experience of 'the more of God, the less of the human Jesus,' or vice versa, and this familiar phenomenon in music serves to render intelligible, feasible, and credible what otherwise would seem paradoxical, if not downright contradictory."[49] The book then elaborates on the

---

47. Pederson, *God, Creation, and All That Jazz*, 18.

48. This chapter also contains her most pointed expression of feminist theology; see below.

49. Peacocke and Pederson, *Music of Creation*, 41.

theme of Pederson's previous work: linking jazz improvisation to a conception of God and human beings as "co-improvisers, embellishing on God's theme of grace, freedom, and love for all creation."[50] Practice as it pertains to both music and the Christian life flows naturally from this premise, and from there it is a short step to modeling the "ensemble of the church . . . after a middle-school jazz band rehearsal."[51] What follows this develops the analogy, focusing especially on risk-taking, the parallels between learning a language and learning how to improvise, and the balance between individuality and collaboration. The final point of contact between music and theology summarizes and extends Begbie's view on the theological implications of music's finitude.

In her first book, Pederson's writing draws in nearly equal parts from her personal experiences and her interaction with other theologians. The result is more narrative than systematic, sometimes resulting in underdeveloped assertions. Furthermore, her approach to jazz lacks depth, relying too heavily on Paul F. Berliner's *Thinking in Jazz: The Infinite Art of Improvisation*, using supportive quotes from jazz musicians as opposed to entering into conversation with them. In fact, her dialogues with process and feminist theologians are more involved than her interaction with music. In what was presumably her portion of *The Music of Creation*, Pederson extends her use of jazz improvisation, but, like Begbie, still holds back from any extended engagement with any jazz musicians of note. That being said, her works raise important issues concerning the doctrines of God and creation and place her among the few theologians who have ventured an extended exploration of the theological implications of jazz and improvisation.

*Assessment and Projections*
Using analogy as a means of approaching the intersection between theology and music is certainly rarer, if not novel, in comparison with employing musical aesthetics. Judging from the

50. Ibid., 50.
51. Ibid., 55.

works considered above, it has the potential to be a fruitful endeavor. Even as a foil, as in the case of Young's work, musical analogy demonstrates the ability to sharpen theological insights, correcting logocentric and visual-conceptual myopias. As a method, musical analogy has almost unlimited potential when applied to areas of theology with which it shares common systems of relations. Unlike the aesthetic approach, however, this approach will never be able to raise music above the status of dialogue partner.

## *Feminist Deconstruction and Reconstruction*

As noted above, feminism remains at present the only deconstructive/reconstructive approach to the intersection of theology and music. It represents a needed dialogue with the sociological and ideological motives behind the production of music.

### *Heidi Epstein*

In *Melting the Venusberg*, Heidi Epstein employs a hermeneutic of suspicion to historical and contemporary Christian engagement with music before engaging in a feminist reconstruction. One could situate Epstein's endeavor under the heading of aesthetics because, like Viladesau, she is using music as a means of engaging in her enterprise. However, since half of her work is concerned with deconstruction, and her reconstruction is specifically focused on a feminist agenda, it seems fitting to acknowledge its uniqueness in relation to the other studies examined here.

Part one of Epstein's work undertakes the deconstruction of overt and subtle sexism in the history of Christian engagement with music. She begins with the "phallic rage for order," tracing the link between music and the cosmos from Pythagoras, Plato, and Aristotle to the Church Fathers. Music is lauded for its "disembodied Order," sweeping aside its bodily groundings and erotic implications.[52] According to Epstein, the bodily-situated, erotic aspect of music was for the Fathers something "to be

---

52. Epstein, *Melting the Venusberg*, 23.

contained, sterilised, and if nothing else, redirected toward God."[53] She makes the case that, beginning in Augustine and realized in Boethius, music became embodied and engendered as a woman, placed in a subservient position to the word. The following chapter continues the chronological deconstruction through the middle ages and into the twentieth century. Convincing evidence is supplied for the perception of music as a woman: virtuous and chaste as a virgin when conforming to masculine ideals, but whorish, seductive, and emasculating when stepping outside the carefully demarcated bounds of her critics. This research grounds Epstein's critique of contemporary models in the final chapter of part one, culminating in the charge that these models "continue to perpetuate the phallic rage for order in similarly conventional terms of harmony and transcendence, sidestepping once again the messy yet creative potential that music's erotic metaphoricity might afford."[54] Among the first to be critiqued with respect to their view of music are the Protestant theologian Karl Barth and the Roman Catholic theologian Hans Küng. Barth's understanding of Mozart is charged with being too transcendent while Küng's assessment of the same composer fails in the same way in spite of his implicit connection between experiencing Mozart's music and sexuality. Her critiques of other figures provide useful summaries and insights into their endeavors, as seen above.

In the second part of her work, Epstein seeks to construct a feminist theology of music. She begins by investigating the theological implications of the connection between music and sexuality. In her reading of the music of Hildegard of Bingen, Hildegard assigns "a redemptive role to the female body,"[55] focuses on the incarnation as opposed to the disembodied, and holds to a Christology where Christ is "God's music-made-flesh" in addition to being the word-made-flesh.[56] Suzanne Cusick's lesbian musicology provides a more direct avenue for Epstein's

---

53. Ibid., 26.
54. Ibid., 59.
55. Ibid., 122.
56. Ibid., 126.

approach: Cusick's "redefinition" of sexuality through music and "minus its usual phallocentric trappings,"[57] when linked to a conception of Christ-as-lover, results in a spiritual transcendence "achieved through the most sensual, polymorphously sexual, means."[58] The following chapter primarily interacts with a narrative in which the nuns in the convent of Santa Cristina della Fondazza in Bologna defied their Archbishop's prohibition on modern music via political and familial connections. Noting the musical success and notoriety gained by these nuns, and keeping the connection between music and the erotic in mind, Epstein sees a melting of the barrier between them and the courtesans of the time. She concludes,

> The clerics' tactics and the nuns' disobedience demonstrate that music's theological significance lies not in its incarnation of harmony and order—divine, cosmic, or human—but precisely in the *"promiscuity" and disintegration* which it breeds; in its disorderly conduct of "power, pleasure, and intimacy" between willing (or not so willing) bodies.[59]

This theme is then elaborated in the next chapter in Epstein's examination of African traditions combining music, dance, sexuality, and spirituality. She then picks up the motif of abjection begun in the previous chapter and considers the confrontational performance practices of AIDS activist Diamanda Gala. Gala is a "postmodern woman-mystic [who] immerses herself in abjection in order adequately to imitate Christ's cruciform plea for justice, compassion, and mercy."[60] Epstein lauds Gala's music as a rebuttal of naive attempts to affirm harmonic order as an answer to pain and suffering.

Stoltzfus rightly points out that Epstein's project relies on the perception of music as being imitative of the body, allowing her to draw lines between it and Christ's Passion. He suggests that her approach in fact shares a similar methodology with Schleiermacher's, in that they both share "a Romantically appropriated

57. Ibid., 131.
58. Ibid., 133.
59. Ibid., 145. Italics in original.
60. Ibid., 176.

expression theory of art."[61] Even if this is in fact the case, it would be difficult to deny that Epstein's program veers sharply from Schleiermacher's in its feminist outlook, explicit treatment of sexuality in music, and its concerted effort to deconstruct the notion of music as a representation of disembodied order.

The first portion of Epstein's work provides a much-needed correction to conceptions of music overlooking music's embodied nature and parallels with human sexuality. However, in spite of her early insistence that her work will not "unilaterally reject"[62] the models she critiques, as she carries out her project it appears that in fact she does. In other words, her project rightly discerns an imbalance in past and present engagement between Christian theology and music, but her reconstructive project is not so much a corrective as an alternative. By consistently rejecting the validity of masculine understandings of music and sexuality, she has left no ground for a rapprochement. This is pronounced in the near absence of ecclesiology from the project.

*Ann Pederson*

As we have seen above, Pederson's approach does not share Epstein's lack of ecclesial application; she actively suggests ways in which her insights can be adapted in the life of the church. Pederson shares, though perhaps to a lesser degree, Epstein's feminist/deconstructionist agenda. It is the most pronounced in the fourth chapter of *God, Creation and All That Jazz*: "The Blues: An Affirmation That Life Still Swings." Appealing to feminist and liberationist thought, Pederson seeks to deconstruct the substitutionary theory of the atonement on the grounds that it has led and continues to lead to the sanction of violence against women and the vulnerable by glorifying Jesus' suffering. Seeking an alternative, she turns to the story, "Sonny's Blues" by James Baldwin, as well as the Afro-American blues tradition, to argue for resistance and transformation in the face of evil and suffering. For Pederson, jazz improvisation

---

61. Stoltzfus, *Theology as Performance*, 14.
62. Epstein, *Melting the Venusberg*, 14.

encapsulates this response: the jazz musician reacts and plays on through the hardships of life.

Like Epstein, Pederson does not leave space for redemption or re-appropriation of the things she rejects. The line connecting the substitutionary theory of atonement to the perpetration of violence effectively outlaws its proponents.

*Assessment and Projections*

Above, I pointed out the weakness of the feminist approach to the intersection of theology in music with respect to a lack of space for rapprochement. This need not be a fatal flaw; it can be solved from within or from without. To solve the problem from within, feminist authors need to clarify how previous models can be resituated in light of the ones they propose. It is not enough to claim that one does not intend to abandon or jettison previous models, especially when the rhetoric points in precisely the opposite direction. To solve the problem from without, those being critiqued need first to acknowledge the critiques being made and then find a way of responding appropriately.

Looking ahead, it is possible that other marginalized voices will join in the task of ferreting out injustices in the narratives of theology and music, perhaps providing new alternatives. Sometimes critiques must be pointed and sharp, but it is to be hoped that ultimately harmony will triumph over cacophony.

## *Conclusion*

While it does not present a unified front, there can be little doubt that a new field is arising from the dialogue between music and theology in light of recent publications. This field represents an intensification, explication, and expansion of the long history of encounters between the two disciplines. Musical aesthetics, analogy, and feminism provide significantly different approaches to the task, but I do not believe they need to be mutually exclusive. This survey has highlighted representative works in the field, but there remain many works to consider, some just outside of its scope. Hopefully critical mass will soon be attained and an important, if still fledgling, field of study will draw a new generation of scholars to aid in the ongoing renewal of the theological enterprise.

*Bibliography*

Begbie, Jeremy S. *Resounding Truth: Christian Wisdom in the World of Music*. Engaging Culture. Grand Rapids: Baker Academic, 2007.

———. *Theology, Music and Time*. Cambridge Studies in Christian Doctrine. Cambridge: Cambridge University Press, 2000.

———. *Voicing Creation's Praise: Towards a Theology of the Arts*. Edinburgh: T. & T. Clark, 1991.

Blackwell, Albert L. "Review of *Theology, Music and Time*." In *Journal of Religion* 18 (2002) 473–74.

———. *The Sacred in Music*. Louisville: Westminster John Knox, 1999.

Brown, Frank Burch. "Aesthetics, Music, and Theology: A Review of Current Literature." *The Arts in Religious and Theological Studies* 13, no. 2 (2001) 32–35.

Bychkov, Oleg V. "Review of *Theology and the Arts: Encountering God through Music, Art, and Rhetoric*." *Modern Theology* 17 (2001) 516–18.

Epstein, Heidi. *Melting the Venusberg: A Feminist Theology of Music*. New York: Continuum, 2004.

Gentner, Dedre. "Analogy." In *A Companion to Cognitive Science*, edited by William Bechtel, George Graham, and D. A. Balota, 107–13. Malden, MA: Blackwell, 1998.

Howison, Jamie. *God's Mind in That Music: Theological Explorations through the Music of John Coltrane.* Eugene, OR: Cascade, 2012.

Leaver, Robin A. "Motive and Motif in the Church Music of Johann Sebastian Bach." *Theology Today* 63 (2006) 38–47.

McBrien, Richard P. *Catholicism.* 2 vols. Minneapolis: Winston, 1980.

Peacocke, Arthur, and Ann Pederson. *The Music of Creation.* Theology and the Sciences. Minneapolis: Fortress, 2006.

Pederson, Ann. *God, Creation, and All That Jazz: A Process of Composition and Improvisation.* St. Louis: Chalice, 2001.

Rivera, Benito V. *German Music Theory in the Early 17th Century: The Treatises of Johannes Lippius.* Studies in Musicology. Ann Arbor, MI: UMI Research Press, 1980.

Stapert, Calvin. *A New Song for an Old World: Musical Thought in the Early Church.* The Calvin Institute of Christian Worship Liturgical Studies Series. Grand Rapids: Eerdmans, 2007.

Stoltzfus, Philip E. *Theology as Performance: Music, Aesthetics, and God in Western Thought.* New York: T. & T. Clark, 2006.

Viladesau, Richard. *Theological Aesthetics: God in Imagination, Beauty, and Art.* New York: Oxford University Press, 1999.

———. *Theology and the Arts: Encountering God through Music, Art and Rhetoric.* New York: Paulist, 2000.

Young, Frances. *The Art of Performance: Towards a Theology of Holy Scripture.* London: Darton, Longman & Todd, 1990.

## The Life and Career of Spinoza:
## A Lesson in Biblical Interpretation

David I. Yoon
McMaster Divinity College, Hamilton, ON, Canada

### Introduction

The current state of biblical interpretation, however one views it, has been highly influenced by the scholarship of Baruch Spinoza (1632–1677). He is certainly considered to be one of the catalysts of the Enlightenment, or at least one who laid the groundwork for the Enlightenment to take place. Much of his methodology in interpreting the biblical text resulted in what we currently call historical criticism,[1] characterized by extreme skepticism of the miraculous and supernatural, and focus on matters of faith and morality over historical precision. Although his *Ethics* is probably the most famous of his works, much of his biblical hermeneutical philosophy comes from his *Theological-Political Treatise*.[2] Due to the focus and limits of this article, I will confine my study to his latter work, focusing on his philosophy of biblical interpretation.

### Brief Biography

Understanding Spinoza's life and experiences is crucial if one would understand the motivations for his methodology of biblical interpretation. But the social, political, and religious

---

1. Frampton, *Spinoza*, 14.
2. I have used the edition of Spinoza's works in Morgan, *Spinoza: Complete Works*. Cf. Yovel, *Spinoza and Other Heretics*, 2:3, who confirms that the *Theological-Political Treatise* is where we get his ideas of biblical hermeneutics.

conditions into which he was born are also very important for understanding the ideas that drove him. For purposes of understanding Spinoza's personal motivations, I will briefly review his birth and early life, including the social, political, and religious conditions into which he was born, as well as circumstances in his adult life that led to his writing career.[3]

Baruch Spinoza was born on 24 November 1632, his name meaning "blessed one" in Hebrew. The name he went by as a child was Bento, Portuguese for "blessed." The Spanish Inquisition was taking place around this time, resulting in many Spanish and Portuguese Jews relocating to Amsterdam, including Spinoza's father and mother (Miguel/Michael de Espinoza and Hana Debora, Miguel's second wife), where they could practice their Jewish faith freely, in contrast to many Jews who had posed as Roman Catholics to be spared persecution back home in Portugal.[4] Those who feigned Catholic belief while still holding to the Jewish faith were called Portuguese Marranos. Yovel notes how the Marranos had a significant impact upon Spinoza's own religious reflections.[5] While Spinoza's early childhood is not heavily documented,[6] it appears that the genesis of his philosophy was when he witnessed, at an early age, the oppressive nature of religious orthodoxy upon its adherents. One experience in particular, when young Bento (as he was presumably called) was not yet ten years old, involved a Spanish convert to Judaism named Uriel d'Acosta, with whom he was acquainted.[7] Uriel yearned to learn of the background to his new Jewish faith, but ended up challenging, or rather was accused of "insulting," the authority of the synagogue leaders, who subsequently excommunicated him from the community. Sometime later, d'Acosta testified that he was publicly flogged in conjunction with his

---

3. For more extensive biography, see Frampton, *Spinoza*, esp. 43–198; Gullan-Whur, *Within Reason*; Klever, "Spinoza's Life and Works"; Yovel, *Spinoza and Other Heretics*, esp. vol. 1.
4. Gullan-Whur, *Within Reason*, 5–6.
5. Yovel, *Spinoza and Other Heretics*, esp. 1:15–39. See also Gullan-Whur, *Within Reason*, 8–14.
6. Gullan-Whur, *Within Reason*, 38.
7. Cf. Strauss, *Spinoza's Critique of Religion*, 53–63.

excommunication, and in the end d'Acosta committed suicide.[8] This series of events undoubtedly had a significant impact upon young Bento, who was naturally peaceable and avoided confrontation, and he ended up despising the authoritarian tyranny of the religious leaders of the day.

Spinoza himself was excommunicated from his religious community on 27 July 1656, when he was about 23 years of age.[9] The excommunication read as follows: "That no one should communicate with him, neither in writing, nor accord him any favor nor stay with him under the same roof nor within four cubits in his vicinity; nor shall he read any treatise composed or written by him."[10] Rabbi Morteira, who was acquainted with both Spinoza's father and grandfather, was purportedly one of the representatives to excommunicate him. There were others with him in this charge, and Spinoza was the quietest and least heretical among them. Gullan-Whur states: "His muted insolence was neither standard youthful questioning nor outright heresy."[11] The religious authorities most likely banned Spinoza from public assembly due to his "sinisterly calm demeanor suggest[ing] a rational ground-clearing of the mind."[12] However, it does not seem that this excommunication affected Spinoza much, at least, it does not appear to have made him seek revenge directly. He simply changed his name from Bento/Baruch to Benedictus (latinizing it), symbolizing a shift in his religious allegiance, if he ever had one.[13]

We need to be aware of several others of Spinoza's experiences in adult life if we wish to understand the fuel that drove his passion for writing his books. He began writing *Theological-*

---

8. Gullan-Whur, *Within Reason*, 37–38.
9. For a more extensive description of this, see Kasher and Biderman, "Why was Baruch de Spinoza Excommunicated?" 51–99. Essentially, they state that outside philosophies (e.g., Cartesian and Quaker) resulted in his banishment. But they admit there are no primary sources that confirm the actual reason.
10. Ibid., 60.
11. Gullan-Whur, *Within Reason*, 68.
12. Ibid.
13. Ibid., 72.

*Political Treatise* (setting aside the writing of *Ethics*, which was partially complete) around 1664 (he was about 31) during a three-sided dispute involving the English, Dutch, and Germans. Dungan writes: "He saw it [the writing of *Theological-Political Treatise*] as his contribution to the struggle for democracy and liberalism in his adoptive country. Little did he suspect the disastrous consequences that would ensue after it was published."[14] His involvement with politics was related to a friendship he had with Jan de Witt, who was prime minister of the Dutch provinces at that time. De Witt was successful in putting the financial affairs of the country in order, and pushed for political democracy and religious toleration. However, there was still some political unrest, as the majority of the heads of the Dutch states decided not to appoint the prince of Orange as the sovereign of the state and instead wanted to move towards being a republic.

In 1668, Spinoza's friend and disciple, Adrian Koerbagh, was being tried in an ecclesiastical court for promoting atheism and hedonism. Koerbagh, who was a successful physician, was questioned about his relationship with Spinoza, and eventually was convicted of heresy. He received several punishments, including cutting off his right thumb (so he could never practice medicine again), having his tongue bored through with a red hot iron (so he could never talk again), being fined 6,000 florins (so he would be financially ruined), and finally receiving a thirty-year prison sentence. He died after serving only a year of his sentence.[15] One could only imagine the effect this treatment had upon Spinoza, particularly as he was writing his *Treatise* during this time.

It was also around this time that Spinoza's friend de Witt got into trouble with both the English and the French, resulting in the possibility of another war. The Dutch responded to the threat by reinstating the Prince of Orange as the national sovereign and sending him to make peace with the English. While de Witt's career was on the brink of extinction, Spinoza's *Treatise* was published and went on the market. Since it was basically a

---

14. Dungan, *History of the Synoptic Problem*, 205.
15. Ibid., 205–6.

treatise against all things orthodox and monarchal, there was much dissension over it, to say the least. De Witt's attempt to suppress it was unsuccessful, and subsequent translations into French, German, and English resulted. Dungan notes that the work resulted in a "violent reaction,"[16] part of which was the termination of de Witt from office and his subsequent imprisonment, along with his brother Cornelius (who was heavily involved in the Dutch military with Jan), since they were known associates of Spinoza. On 20 August 1672, a mob stormed into the prison where the de Witt brothers were held and killed them, dragging their bodies into the streets where the attackers hacked them into pieces. When Spinoza heard news of this, he flew into an uncontrollable rage and attempted to go to the scene, but his landlord successfully locked him in and probably saved his life.[17] Spinoza than decided he would seclude himself from political life, and lived the rest of his life in near isolation. He once declined a professorship offered by Karl Ludwig at the newly founded University of Heidelberg, and instead, finished writing *Ethics*, despite his uncertainty of how it would be received.

A couple of years later (1674), Spinoza learned that his old friend Frans Van den Enden had been hanged in France, due to "the collapse of a utopian scheme there."[18] This depressed Spinoza even more, ultimately crushing his "republican optimism,"[19] and his deteriorating health resulted in his death on 21 February 1677, at the young age of 45. One can (and should) easily empathize with Spinoza after understanding the horrific persecution he and his friends and colleagues endured. This set the stage for what developed as Spinoza's philosophy of religion, especially his philosophy of biblical interpretation.

---

16. Ibid., 206.
17. Morgan, Introduction to "Political Treatise," 676. He contends that the facts surrounding Spinoza's relationship with de Witt may be disputed, whether he personally knew him or not, but most seem to think that they had a friendship of some sort, cf. for example, Gullan-Whur, *Within Reason*, 58–60.
18. Dungan, *History of the Synoptic Problem*, 207.
19. Ibid., 207.

## Spinoza's Philosophy and Methodology

Spinoza's experiences, as described in the previous section, are critical to understanding his philosophy of biblical interpretation and, in general, religion. Dungan suggests two aspects of his philosophical vision that are important for understanding Spinoza. First is his "profound moral rage." Dungan writes:

> As a Marrano Jew whose heritage included two hundred years of brutal persecution, first in Spain and then in Portugal, Spinoza and his fellow Amsterdam Marrano Jews were only too aware of the precariousness of their existence in the presence of autocratic Christian sovereigns and powerful and prejudiced Christian preachers. Centuries of vicious treatment, encouraged and led by Christian clergy, bred in many Jews, including Baruch de Spinoza, an all-consuming rage.[20]

This is certainly evident in the preface of his *Theological-Political Treatise*, as well as the entire work, where he proceeds to destroy "the entire medieval religious worldview, repeatedly putting one thing in its place: the commandment to love God and *love your neighbor*" (italics original).[21] Details of this attitude will be given throughout this paper.

The second aspect of his philosophical vision is his ability and willingness to see beyond the claims of Judeo-Christianity toward a new vision of the universe, a freedom that was not at all common during this period. Dungan writes: "In Spinoza and other Jews, the behavior of both the hated Spanish monarchs and Jesuit Inquisition, as well as the miserable hypocrisy of the *conversos* [i.e. Jewish converts to Roman Catholicism for the sake of avoiding persecution], produced an utter skepticism regarding all religious claims."[22] This new vision of the universe was partly based on the views of Descartes, who skeptically questioned anything one could not know with certainty, including metaphysical and theological constructs. "No hidden agenda

---

20. Ibid., 208.
21. Ibid., 209.
22. Ibid.

permitted here; no illicit logical leaps."[23] But he also denied Descartes' idea that "God" was a part of "basic knowledge," and contended that "nature" actually constituted basic knowledge. Nevertheless, Descartes was certainly a huge influence upon the development of Spinoza's philosophical worldview.

Spinoza's methodology could be construed as a type of historical criticism, but it was essentially a polemic against the religious hierarchy of his day:

> It is commonly believed that the historical investigation of the Bible pioneered by Spinoza and [Richard] Simon represented a major breakthrough for the spirit of scientific objectivity, releasing the Bible to speak for itself after centuries of dogmatic allegorical exegesis in medieval Roman Catholicism, and the equally doctrinaire readings of the Bible employed by Protestant scholasticism.[24]

One of the commonly understood fruits of the Enlightenment was the development of an *objective, scientific* method of study, particularly of the Bible; many of its students wanted to study the Bible outside of dogma or theological agenda, stripped of its doctrinal bias and understood in strictly historical terms. However, it is clear that Spinoza's methodology was far from objective and passionless; in fact, there was a different agenda for his historical-critical method, especially seen in his *Theological-Political Treatise*. Dungan states that "the method of historical criticism was utilized by Spinoza as an ally in the struggle against the tyranny of dogma (both Jewish and Christian) and also to identify the political ideology that was its ultimate rationale."[25] He also claims that Spinoza—along with other Enlightenment scholars such as Thomas Hobbes, John Locke, David Hume, Gottfried Wilhelm von Leibniz, and Immanuel Kant—used biblical criticism *"as a weapon to destroy or at least discredit the traditional metaphysics of Christianity and Judaism."*[26] Yovel also states: "His biblical hermeneutics is not only an independent science in itself; it is also—and primarily—a

---

23. Ibid., 210.
24. Ibid., 198.
25. Ibid., 199.
26. Ibid. (italics original).

weapon in combating historical religion and a vehicle in constructing a purified substitute for it."[27]

## Summary of Spinoza's Works

While Spinoza is widely known for his *Ethics*, which is a "comprehensive account of his philosophical system,"[28] he also wrote several books dealing with other philosophical and political issues, many of which were left incomplete at the time of his death. His *Principles of Cartesian Philosophy and Metaphysical Thoughts* is probably his most significant philosophical work outside of *Ethics* and the *Theological-Political Treatise*, outlining the philosophy of Rene Descartes. That Spinoza was a solitary rebel is a bit of a misconception, as he was part of a group of Cartesian philosophers who participated in this revolution, including Frans (or Franciscus) Van den Enden, Lodewijk Meyer, Johan Bouwmeester, Pieter Balling, Simon de Vries, and Jarig Jelles.[29] He also wrote a Hebrew grammar, reflective of his rationalist belief that interpreting Scripture requires knowledge of its original language, which he believed to be living and human, rather than a sacred, holy, mysterious system.[30]

He also wrote a few shorter works, including *Treatise on the Emendation of the Intellect*, which is the earliest record of Spinoza's professional philosophical writing, most likely written after his excommunication in 1656 and his subsequent involvement in the Collegiate (an eclectic group of religious thinkers who met regularly to discuss various issues of religion and to encourage free thinking). It outlines three major aspects of his blooming philosophy: (1) the value of scientific reason and knowledge of nature, (2) the superiority of deductive and intuitive reason over imagination and sensation, and (3) requirements for definition, distinguishing independent essences from dependent and contingent ones.[31] There is also his *Short Treatise on*

---

27. Yovel, *Spinoza and Other Heretics*, 2:3.
28. Morgan, Introduction to "Ethics," 213.
29. Morgan, Introduction to "Principles of Cartesian Philosophy," 108.
30. Morgan, Introduction to "Hebrew Grammar," 584.
31. Morgan, Introduction to "Treatise on the Emendation of the Intellect," 1–2.

*God, Man, and His Well-Being*, which discusses the origin of things and a first cause, including various proofs of God's existence.[32] It is safe to say that his philosophy was incomplete at this time, and that a more comprehensive philosophy would be found in *Ethics*.

He expanded on his political ideas in his *Political Treatise*, which became a sort of addendum as the final five chapters of his *Theological-Political Treatise*, strictly focusing on political issues. Furthermore, many of the letters he wrote to his friends and colleagues have been preserved, which reveal more of Spinoza's personal motivations and thoughts.

Due to the nature and limits of this article, I will spend the majority of space in reviewing his *Theological-Political Treatise*, which is more related to his view of biblical interpretation than his other works (though *Ethics* is certainly a more comprehensive work), and compare relevant sections of his other works where appropriate.

*Purposes for Writing* Theological-Political Treatise

Spinoza's purposes in writing this treatise were explicated in a letter to his friend Henry Oldenburg. The following is a short excerpt of this letter:

> I am now writing a treatise on my views regarding Scripture. The reasons that move me to do so are these:
> 1. The prejudices of the theologians. For I know that these are the main obstacles which prevent men from giving their minds to philosophy. So I apply myself to exposing such prejudices and removing them from the minds of sensible people.
> 2. The opinion of me held by the common people, who constantly accuse me of atheism. I am driven to avert this accusation, too, as far as I can.

---

32. Morgan, Introduction to "Short Treatise," 31–32.

3. The freedom to philosophise and to say what we think. This I want to vindicate completely, for here it is in every way suppressed by the excessive authority and egotism of preachers.[33]

Again, the heavy libertarian leanings of Spinoza are evident: the freedom to think, the freedom to choose one's own beliefs, the freedom to question and ponder.[34] We must remember that while this kind of thinking may not be as radical for us today (having gone through such revolutions as the civil rights movement and the feminist movement in recent decades in North America), it was certainly something that was derided during Spinoza's time.

His *Theological-Political Treatise* contains twenty chapters, fifteen on theology and five on politics. In the following section, I will summarize some of Spinoza's main points relevant to his theory and understanding of biblical interpretation. Special focus will be given to chapter 7, "Of the Interpretation of Scripture." But before doing so, I want to review some preliminary remarks made by Spinoza in his preface that will further elucidate his intent.[35]

First, it must be noted that Spinoza spurned the miraculous, attributing belief in the miraculous to superstition. He stated that miracles are to be interpreted naturally, as closely as possible.[36] He then attributed the source of "superstition" to fear: "It is fear, then, that engenders, preserves and fosters superstition."[37] He also writes: "For it arises not from reason but from emotion, and

---

33. Spinoza, "Letter 30," 844. See also Strauss, *Spinoza's Critique of Religion*, 111–12. Strauss also recognizes that Spinoza's ultimate purpose in writing this treatise is with "the freedom of philosophizing" (112).

34. As another example of this, in the preface to *Theological-Political Treatise*, he writes: "... everyone should be allowed freedom of judgment and the right to interpret the basic tenet of his faith as he thinks fit, and that the moral value of a man's creed should be judged only from his works. In this way all men would be able to obey God wholeheartedly and freely, and only justice and charity would be held in universal esteem" (393).

35. Dungan notes that the preface in this work reveals "all of the passionate concerns within Spinoza's heart more clearly than any other writing of his" (Dungan, *History of the Synoptic Problem*, 217).

36. Spinoza, "Theological-Political Treatise," 455.

37. Ibid., 388.

emotion of the most powerful kind. So men's readiness to fall victim to any kind of superstition makes it correspondingly difficult to persuade them to adhere to one and the same kind."[38] He defines miracles as "stories of unusual occurrences in Nature, adapted to the beliefs and judgment of the historians who recorded them."[39] So while Spinoza criticized the religiously orthodox for their presuppositions, it appears Spinoza's own presupposition was a naturalistic worldview. This will continue to be evident throughout his work, as we will see.

It is important to note Spinoza's purpose statement in the preface:

> This, then, is the main point which I have sought to establish in this treatise. For this purpose my most urgent task has been to indicate the main false assumptions that prevail regarding religion—that is, the relics of man's ancient bondage—and then again the false assumptions regarding the right of civil authorities.[40]

These false assumptions were related to one of Spinoza's bigger contentions, in fact, the biggest criticism he had against religious orthodoxy, not surprising given his experiences as outlined briefly above. He wrote: "I have often wondered that men who make a boast of professing the Christian religion, which is a religion of love, joy, peace, temperance and honest dealing with all men, should quarrel so fiercely and display the bitterest hatred toward one another day by day, so that these latter characteristics make known a man's creed more readily than the former."[41] He saw a huge inconsistency between what

---

38. Ibid., 389.
39. Ibid., 457.
40. Ibid., 390.
41. Spinoza, "Theological-Political Treatise," 390. He also extends this idea to the introduction to his seventh chapter: "On every side we hear men saying that the Bible is the Word of God, teaching mankind true blessedness, or the path to salvation. But the facts are quite at variance with their words, for people in general seem to make no attempt whatsoever to live according to the Bible's teachings. We see that nearly all men parade their own ideas as God's Word, their chief aim being to compel others to think as they do, while using religion as a pretext. We see, I say, that the chief concern of theologians on the whole has been to extort from Holy Scripture their own arbitrary invented ideas, for

they professed and how they acted—in essence, he detested their hypocrisy. He also contended that his contemporaries taught little more than the philosophies of Aristotle and Plato, rather than unveiling the mysteries of "divine light."[42] He wrote: "It was not enough for them to share in the delusions of the Greeks: they have sought to represent the prophets as sharing in these same delusions."[43] By using rhetorical language, he was aiming to break down the perceived infallibility of the religious authorities and give power back to individuals to think freely for themselves.

*Principles for Interpreting Scripture*

Now that I have expounded the purposes and causes of Spinoza's theological ideas, and more specifically his *Theological-Political Treatise*, I will review a few key points he made regarding his view of biblical interpretation. First is his approach to interpreting Scripture. He writes: "Now to put it briefly, I hold that the method of interpreting Scripture is no different from the method of interpreting Nature, and is in fact in complete accord with it."[44] This results in a naturalistic interpretation of supernatural occurrences in Scripture, resulting from Spinoza's pantheistic view of God as synonymous to nature.[45] But with respect to actual principles, he briefly states that interpreting Nature involves a deductive method, using only principles from Nature to draw conclusions about Nature, without any prejudices or

---

which they claim divine authority . . . Now if men were really sincere in what they profess with regard to Holy Scripture, they would conduct themselves quite differently; they would not be racked by so much quarrelling and such bitter feuding, and they would not be gripped by this blind and passionate desire to interpret Scripture and to introduce innovations in religion. On the contrary, they would never venture to accept as Scriptural doctrine what was not most clearly taught in Scripture itself" (456).

42. Ibid., 391.
43. Ibid.
44. Ibid., 457.
45. See Keener, *Miracles*, 114–15, for a concise critique of Spinoza's naturalism/pantheism. He suggests that Spinoza's assumption that divine nature is identical to natural law is subject to critique, in light of "theological and philosophic readings of contemporary physics" (115).

assumptions being held. The same applies to Scripture.[46] He writes:

> In this way—that is, by allowing no other principles or data for the interpretation of Scripture and study of its contents except those that can be gathered only from Scripture itself and from a historical study of Scripture—steady progress can be made without any danger of error, and one can deal with matters that surpass our understanding with no less confidence than those matters which are known to us by the natural light of reason.[47]

So the approach to studying Scripture is a rationalistic deductive approach, gathering all the relevant data and drawing appropriate conclusions. "Therefore, knowledge of all these things—that is, of almost all the contents of Scripture—must be sought from Scripture alone, just as knowledge of Nature must be sought from Nature itself."[48] Again, he later writes: "Therefore all knowledge of Scripture must be sought from Scripture alone."[49] This sounds like the Protestant, no less Reformed, principle that *Scripture interprets Scripture*.[50]

A second point in interpretation is what he calls the "universal rule" for interpretation, namely, "to ascribe no teaching to Scripture that is not clearly established from studying it closely."[51] Again, this is in line with his deductive approach, the idea that Scripture interprets Scripture. It agrees with the Enlightenment and rationalist philosophy of ascertaining truth according to deductive reasoning. He outlines three general principles for interpretation.

First is the primacy of the original languages, particularly the Hebrew language. He states that "we should be able to investigate, from established linguistic usage, all the possible meanings of any passage."[52] He not only applies the influence of

---

46. With specific referent to ideas such as inspiration and the supernatural.
47. Spinoza, "Theological-Political Treatise," 457.
48. Ibid.
49. Ibid., 458.
50. Walther, "Spinoza's Critique of Miracles," 280.
51. Spinoza, "Theological-Political Treatise," 458.
52. Ibid.

the Hebrew language for the Old Testament, but also the New Testament, since the New Testament writers were Hebrews and their idiom was Hebraic, even if it was written in Greek. Thus, it is not surprising that he published a Hebrew grammar, since he deemed it to be important in interpretation.

A second principle of interpretation that Spinoza advocates is the idea of categorizing and listing various statements (or pronouncements) together in terms of their degree of clarity. He writes: "The pronouncements made in each book should be assembled and listed under headings, so that we can thus have to hand all the texts that treat of the same subject."[53] He asserts that all the "obscure" or difficult statements, even apparently contradictory ones, should be categorized together. Obscure statements are those, he defines, which are difficult to determine "according to the difficulty with which the meaning can be elicited from the context, and not according to the degree of difficulty with which its truth can be perceived by reason."[54] So he affirms that obscure passages are not those that we may disagree with, but those in which it is difficult to ascertain the meaning. He affirms again that interpreters should put aside their own prejudices and assumptions and seek to find an objective meaning in the text.[55]

An example he gives of this is in the statements of Moses,[56] "God is fire" and "God is jealous," presumably taken from various passages in the Pentateuch where God is manifested in fire (since he gives no precise references to these statements and the precise statement "God is fire" cannot be located). He claims that linguistically, these statements are clear, even though the literal meaning of these statements may be contrary to "the

---

53. Ibid.
54. Ibid.
55. Ibid. He writes: "In order to avoid confusion between true meaning and truth of fact, the former must be sought simply from linguistic usage, or from a process of reasoning that looks to no other basis than Scripture."
56. Interestingly, here he cites Moses as the author, although he was known for his wholesale denial of Mosaic authorship of the Pentateuch, since knowledge of this is unavailable directly in Scripture (cf. Strauss, *Spinoza's Critique of Religion*, 142–44).

natural light of reason," as he states.[57] The basis by which one would have to take these statements literally is in comparison with other statements of Moses. So he writes: "Therefore the question as to whether Moses did or did not believe that God is fire must in no wise be decided by the rationality or irrationality of the belief, but solely from other pronouncements of Moses."[58] Based on this principle, Spinoza concludes that since other pronouncements of Moses state that God is unlike physical or tangible things and has no semblance of such, the statement "God is fire" must be taken metaphorically. However, the interpreter should also investigate the linguistic phenomenon of the meaning of "fire" and see whether this term (in the Hebrew) is used metaphorically in the same sense in other places. Spinoza finds that it is (e.g., Job 31:12), and so the two statements "God is fire" and "God is jealous" are one and the same.[59] Further, whether we believe it or not, since there are no statements to state that God is without emotions or passions, we must believe that (at the very least) Moses believed that God is jealous. Whether we believe it or not is a separate discussion, as Spinoza writes: "For, as we have shown, it is not permissible for us to manipulate Scripture's meaning to accord with our reason's dictates and our preconceived opinions; all knowledge of the Bible is to be sought from the Bible alone."[60] Taken at face value, Spinoza's principles align quite nicely with many of the tenets established during the Reformation, such as *sola scriptura* and the idea that *Scripture interprets Scripture*. But again, it is evident that his intent was dissonant to what the Reformers had in mind.

A third principle of Spinoza relates to the historical aspect of biblical interpretation. "Finally, our historical study should set forth the circumstances relevant to all the extant books of the prophets, giving the life, character and pursuits of the author of

---

57. Spinoza, "Theological-Political Treatise," 458–59.
58. By "rational" and "irrational," I am interpreting these words to be more closely related to *believable/unbelievable* rather than *logical/illogical*.
59. Spinoza, "Theological-Political Treatise," 459.
60. Ibid.

every book, detailing who he was, on what occasion and at what time and for whom and in what language he wrote."[61] This includes investigating the historical background of each book of the Bible, identifying the author and the circumstances in which the author wrote each book, as well as identifying the audience of each book.[62] This also extends to textual criticism (locating textual variants) and a type of canonical study, investigating how each book relates to the canon, and how and why it was received into the canon. In order to recognize the difference between laws and moral teachings, he writes, "it is important to be acquainted with the life, character and interests of the author."[63] But again, this should not be confused with "traditional" grammatical-historical methods of interpretation,[64] as "in Spinoza's hands this slogan [Scripture interprets Scripture] takes on new meaning."[65]

Spinoza was adamant that the outline he proposed for studying Scripture was not only the best way, but the only way, to an accurate understanding of the text. He writes: "We have thus set out our plan for interpreting Scripture, at the same time, demonstrating that this is the only sure road to the discovery of its true meaning."[66] Of course, he is pointing to a deductive reasoning model for his interpretation of Scripture as we have seen from the examples discussed above.

*Practical Implications of Spinoza's Methodology*
After laying out his principles for interpreting Scripture, Spinoza noted some of the practical implications for what he proposed.

61. Ibid.
62. However, this should be distinct from what is traditionally known as discovering authorial intent, since Spinoza's intent was skeptical. Walther writes: "The general consequence of this insight is that one must read all scriptural reports in a critical spirit. That is, in order to understand what really took place, one must first know the views and interest of the narrator, in order not to take the given interpretation for the thing itself" (Walther, "Spinoza's Critique of Miracles," 284).
63. Spinoza, "Theological-Political Treatise," 459.
64. See for example Terry, *Biblical Hermeneutics*, 143; Hirsch, *Validity*, 1–23.
65. Curley, "Notes on a Neglected Masterpiece," 331.
66. Spinoza, "Theological-Political Treatise," 462.

The first implication is that his method "demands a thorough knowledge of the Hebrew language."[67] He posed the question of where this knowledge should be obtained, and stated that the ancients had left insufficient knowledge of the Hebrew language to his contemporaries. He wrote:

> The idiom and modes of speech peculiar to the Hebrew nation have almost all been consigned to oblivion by the ravages of time. So we cannot always discover to our satisfaction all the possible meanings which a particular passage can yield from linguistic usage; and there are many passages where the sense is very obscure and quite incomprehensible although the component words have a clearly established meaning."[68]

Herein lies the skepticism for which Spinoza is known, not only "our inability to present a complete account of the Hebrew language," but also "the further problem presented by the composition and nature of that language."[69] He writes: "This gives rise to so many ambiguities as to render it impossible to devise a method that can teach us with certainty how to discover the true meaning of all Scriptural passages; for apart from the sources of ambiguity that are common to all languages, there are others peculiar to Hebrew which give rise to many ambiguities."[70] He proceeds to list several of these. One ambiguity is a result of the gutturals and the oral nature of the Hebrew language. He states that there may be confusion, for example, between על and אל, since they are so similar. But in most cases, it appears the context would determine which reading fits best. A second source of ambiguity involves the multiple meanings of the conjunctions. However, it may be said that even conjunctions in the Greek have multiple functions, depending on the context in which they are used, so again, context plays an important role in determining meaning.[71] The third ambiguity he claims is the lack of other tenses in the indicative mood of the Hebrew language,

---

67. Ibid., 463.
68. Ibid.
69. Ibid.
70. Ibid.
71. See Porter, *Idioms*, 204–19.

such as the present, past, imperfect, future, and pluperfect. Of course, recent research has shown that the Greek verbal system is more like the Hebrew verbal system than previously thought, with three major aspects that dominate (perfective, imperfective, and stative; compared to the perfect and imperfect aspects in the Hebrew verbal system),[72] and again, context plays a major role in shaping the meaning of the verbal unit.

A couple of other, more significant, ambiguities in the Hebrew language, Spinoza states, are (1) the lack of letters for vowels, and (2) the lack of punctuation and means of emphasis. Of course, we know that the Masoretes were skilled textual critics, but Spinoza states that they were simply "men of later ages [who] added both of these in accordance with their own interpretation of the Bible."[73] However, as Emanuel Tov states, while the Masoretic Text was solidified in the Middle Ages, the shape of the text most likely preceded it by a much earlier tradition.[74] Furthermore, Spinoza simply writes off the Masoretes without seriously interacting with the careful science and art they crafted for preserving the original text as accurately as possible.[75]

It is interesting that though Spinoza begins with some definite assertions about how to interpret Scripture, he concludes with much skepticism regarding its actual possibility. He writes: "These difficulties [noted above], which I undertook to recount, I consider so grave that I have no hesitation in affirming that in many instances we either do not know the true meaning of Scripture or we can do no more than make conjecture."[76] However, he states that the basic meaning of Scripture still can be ascertained, just as one can ascertain the general gist of Euclid without reading it in its original language. Thus, Spinoza boils down the

---

72. See Porter, *Verbal Aspect*, passim; Porter, *Idioms*, 20–49, for lengthy discussion of verbal aspect theory for Hellenistic Greek.
73. Spinoza, "Theological-Political Treatise," 464.
74. Tov, *Textual Criticism*, 23–73, esp. 24–26.
75. See, for example, ibid., 23–73, for a detailed study of the Masoretic Text and how it came about.
76. Spinoza, "Theological-Political Treatise," 466.

basic meaning of Scripture to its moral and ethical components, while its historical and factual aspects are highly questionable.[77]

However, the "plain" statements of Scripture do not reflect this at all, statements such as Jesus stating "I am the way, the truth, and the life," or Paul describing Jesus' resurrection in physical terms. One can understand why Spinoza would hold this conviction, especially considering his life experiences. But to give a concrete example of Spinoza's method of interpretation, the next section will see how he applied his method to actual texts of Scripture.

## *The Application of Spinoza's Hermeneutic*

As stated above, Spinoza believed that only the moral and ethical teachings in Scripture were important, and that historical statements were unreliable, based on some ambiguities in the Hebrew language.[78] Spinoza used a lot of contextual exegesis in his interpretation of texts. His interpretations of two statements in the Sermon on the Mount in particular are given below, illustrating his principles.

### *The Moral Teachings of Jesus*

First, Spinoza takes the statement by Jesus, "Blessed are they that mourn, for they shall be comforted," and asks the (appropriate) question (in the form of a statement), "we do not know

---

77. He writes: "Thus we can conclude that, with the help of such a historical study of Scripture as is available to us, we can readily grasp the meanings of its moral doctrines and be certain of their true sense ... Therefore we have no reason to be unduly anxious concerning the other contents of Scripture; for since for the most part they are beyond the grasp of reason and intellect, they belong to the sphere of the curious rather than the profitable" (ibid., 467).

78. Another proposed difficulty not yet mentioned deals with the possibility that certain books of Scripture (e.g., Matthew and Hebrews) were written in a different language originally, of which we do not have any copies or versions (ibid., 466). However, this is based on mere conjecture (although there may be good reason to believe it to be the case), and reliant upon another assumption, that if there were an original version of Matthew and Hebrews, that the translations are inaccurate renditions of them.

from this text what kind of mourners are meant."[79] In (good) grammatical-contextual examination, he concludes:

> But as Christ thereafter teaches that we should take thought for nothing save only the kingdom of God and His righteousness, which he commends as the highest good (Matth. Ch. 6 v. 33), it follows that by mourners he means only those who mourn for man's disregard of the kingdom of God and His righteousness; for only this can be the cause of mourning for those who love nothing but the kingdom of God, or justice, and utterly despise whatever else fortune has to offer.[80]

While critique of the exact exegesis of this passage is beyond the scope of this paper,[81] Spinoza's words illustrate his use of context to determine the meaning of a seemingly difficult passage or word.

A second example in the Sermon on the Mount that Spinoza provides for illustrating his interpretive principles relates to Matt 5:39, which states, "But if a man strike you on the right cheek, turn to him the left also." He states that if the context were on judges in the role of lawgivers, this command would have violated the law of Moses, which states "an eye for an eye." However, because of the predicating statement by Jesus in Matt 5:17 ("I have not come to abolish the law but to fulfill it"), the difficulty is reconciled by understanding that:

> [Jesus] was not ordaining laws as a lawgiver, but was expounding his teachings as a teacher, because (as we have already shown) he was intent on improving men's minds rather than their external actions. Further, he spoke these words to men suffering under oppression,

---

79. Ibid., 460.
80. Ibid., 460–61.
81. The purpose is not to decide whether Spinoza was a "good" exegete, but to simply illustrate his interpretive process. Here, he simply uses context to determine the specific meaning and application of the word "mourn." Interestingly, he does not go into much depth regarding the original language (whether Hebrew or Greek), a main principle of interpretation.

living in a corrupt commonwealth where justice was utterly disregarded, a commonwealth whose ruin he saw to be imminent.[82]

Here Spinoza again utilizes contextual cues to determine the meaning of a passage that may have come into dispute, showing how an interpreter may resolve a seemingly difficult passage.

An observation should be made at this point that confirms Spinoza's admission that he utilizes his principles of interpretation only for those texts that are of a moral or ethical nature. While he insists that no prejudice or assumption be placed upon the text, he himself assumes that only the moral commands in Scripture are those that are clear, and any historical or factual statements are beyond interpretation. Why he dichotomizes between moral and historical statements for interpretation should be evident already, given the hypocritical and violent persecution of the religious leaders of his day.[83] His motives were clearly spelled out, nowhere more clearly than in the preface to his *Theological-Political Treatise*.[84]

Next we will observe his views on the apostolic authorship of the New Testament epistles and how they impacted his interpretation of these books.

### Apostolic Authorship and Interpretation

While Spinoza was a Jew who focused more on the Hebrew Scriptures than the New Testament, he did interact with the New Testament as well, as we have just seen. Chapter 11 of his *Theological-Political Treatise* is entitled "An enquiry as to whether the Apostles wrote their Epistles as Apostles and prophets, or as teachers. The function of the Apostles is explained."[85] This is in accord with his principle of identifying the

---

82. Spinoza, "Theological-Political Treatise," 461. Again, the point here is not to critique his exegesis, but to illustrate how he applied the principles he provided.

83. See for example Dungan, *History of the Synoptic Problem*, 208: "He clearly felt compelled to take on the theologians and preachers and do whatever he could to break their power, discredit them, and convince people to turn away from them."

84. Ibid., 217.

85. Spinoza, "Theological-Political Treatise," 498–503.

author of each book and the circumstances surrounding their writings (see above). We will evaluate the application of his method in the following paragraphs.

In chapter 1 of *Theological-Political Treatise*, Spinoza contends that prophets did not speak at all times from revelation;[86] based on this understanding, he poses the question: did the apostles write the epistles as prophets (with the express authority from God), or did they write them as teachers (as private individuals)? In other words, he questions whether the epistles are authoritative words of God or whether they are simply teachings of the church leaders.[87] Of course, this is an appropriate investigation for Spinoza, since he establishes the importance of authorial identification as a part of biblical interpretation (see above). Not surprisingly, he contends that the New Testament epistles are not prophecy, for three reasons.

---

86. Ibid., esp. 402–4. He writes: "the Spirit of the Lord was upon a prophet, the Lord poured his Spirit into men, men were filled with the Spirit of God and with the Holy Spirit and so on. They mean merely this, that the prophets were endowed with an extraordinary virtue exceeding the normal, and that they devoted themselves to piety with especial constancy. Furthermore, they perceived the mind and thought of God . . . Therefore the imaginative faculty of the prophets, insofar as it was the instrument for the revelation of God's decrees, could equally well be called the mind of God, and the prophets could be said to have possessed the mind of God. Now the mind of God and his eternal thoughts are inscribed in our minds, too, and therefore we also, in Scriptural language, perceive the mind of God. But since natural knowledge is common to all men, it is not so highly prized, as I have already said, and particularly in the case of the Hebrews, who vaunted themselves above all men—indeed, despising all men, and consequently the sort of knowledge that is common to all men" (402–3). Spinoza's view of prophecy, then, differs from traditional understandings of prophecy, which is viewed as speaking the very words of God (see, e.g., Grudem, *The Gift of Prophecy*, 21–23). Traditional understandings of prophecy, or prophets, claim that the prophet speaks the very words of God, not, as Spinoza claims, simply having the mind of God, which evidently is "inscribed in our [perceivably, everyone's] minds."

87. Baird also notes that he rejected the apostles as the originators of the epistles, but Spinoza does not mention this in this treatise (Baird, *History of New Testament Research*, 1:6).

First, he contends that the style of writing differs significantly from the Old Testament prophetic writings.[88] He notes that it was the "constant practice of the prophets to declare at all points that they were speaking at God's command,"[89] phrases such as "thus saith the Lord," and "the commandment of the Lord," phrases that we do not observe in the New Testament epistles. In contrast to this type of prophetic formula that the Old Testament prophets used to confirm their prophecies, the New Testament prophets seem to relay their own opinions. The example he gives is 1 Cor 7:40, where Paul states his own opinion.

However, Spinoza misunderstands this verse. First, Paul immediately states in the same verse that this "opinion" is from the Spirit of God, and second, the Greek for "opinion" (γνώμη) has more of a sense of maxim than of personal opinion.[90] Furthermore, the omission of the Old Testament prophetic formula does not necessitate the omission of prophecy itself in the New Testament, for a variety of reasons. There is a lack of this formula in general in the New Testament, which would indicate, according to Spinoza's line of thinking, that only a few statements in the New Testament are actual prophecy. This line of thinking would further indicate that the vast majority of statements of Jesus himself are not prophecy.

The second reason Spinoza gives for contending that the epistles are not prophecy is regarding the manner in which the apostles expounded the gospel.[91] He makes the observation that the apostles "everywhere employ argument, so that they seem to be conducting a discussion rather than prophesying. The prophetic writings, on the other hand, contain only dogma and decrees, for they represent God as speaking not like one who reasons, but one who makes decrees issuing from the absolute power of his nature."[92]

---

88. Spinoza, "Theological-Political Treatise," 498.
89. Ibid.
90. Thiselton, *First Epistle to the Corinthians*, 605. See also Louw and Nida, *Lexicon*, who define this lexeme as "that which is purposed or intended, with the implication of judgment or resolve—'purpose, intention,'" §30.67).
91. Spinoza, "Theological-Political Treatise," 499.
92. Ibid.

But this is a narrow view of prophets in the Old Testament. There was a variety of means by which the prophets spoke the word of God. One example is the occasion when Nathan the prophet addressed David about his sin of adultery with Bathsheba (2 Samuel 12) with a fable (or an extended metaphor). This is certainly beyond the categories of "dogma and decrees." Another example comes from the Ten Commandments, which Moses prophesied to the nation of Israel. The fifth commandment is to honor one's father and mother, followed by a *reason*: "that your days may be long, and that it may go well with you in the land that Yahweh your God is giving you" (Deut 5:16). Moses the prophet argues and reasons (hence, God argues and reasons) that honoring one's parents will lead to long life.

The final reason for Spinoza not accepting the epistles to be prophecy is an appeal to reason.[93] He writes:

> I do not absolutely deny that the prophets may have argued from the basis of revelation, but this much I will assert, that the more use the prophets make of logical reasoning, the more closely does their revelatory knowledge approach to natural knowledge, and the surest mark of supernatural knowledge in the prophets is their proclamation of pure dogma, or decrees, or judgment.[94]

The underlying assumption of Spinoza is that revelatory knowledge (i.e., revelation) and natural knowledge (i.e., logic) are absolutely separate kinds of knowledge that do not coincide. He relegates supernatural knowledge to dogma and decrees—which is essentially a presupposition merely asserted without evidence—but this assertion is simply not consistent with other parts of Scripture (using Spinoza's method of authorial identification). Paul argues in his Epistle to the Romans that knowledge of God is evident within all humanity (cf. 1:18–25). While the primary referent of this knowledge is his "invisible attributes" (Rom 1:20), it also by contextual reference includes a moral component, since the subsequent sentences in this discourse say that immorality, that is, "all manner of unrighteousness

---

93. Ibid.
94. Ibid., 500.

(πάσῃ ἀδικίᾳ)" (Rom 1:26–32), is a result of suppressing the knowledge of God. The point I am trying to make is that, using Spinoza's own principles of taking clear language to mean what it means without consideration of whether one believes it or not, Paul advocates a natural knowledge that is moral; in this case, revelatory knowledge and natural knowledge (or revelation and logic) go together.

Spinoza ends his chapter on the apostles with his view of their overall purpose: "This is the object of the Epistles, to teach and exhort men in whatever way each Apostle judged would best strengthen them in religious faith."[95] Spinoza emphasizes (1) the moral component of the faith, and (2) the naturalistic source for this morality.[96]

Again, we must note the inconsistency here, utilizing the principles Spinoza outlines in his previous chapter on interpretation. Paul writes to the Corinthians: "For Christ did not send me to baptize but to preach the gospel, not with words of wisdom, so that the cross of Christ would not lose its power (οὐ γὰρ ἀπέστειλέν με Χριστὸς βαπτίζειν ἀλλὰ εὐαγγελίζεσθαι, οὐκ ἐν σοφίᾳ λόγου, ἵνα μὴ κενωθῇ ὁ σταυρὸς τοῦ Χριστοῦ)" (1 Cor 1:17). What is the gospel that Paul preached? He outlines it in 15:1–13 of the same epistle: it consists of the facts surrounding who Jesus was and what he did, namely his death and resurrection.[97] It appears Paul's *morality* is based on his understanding of *history* (i.e., Jesus' death and resurrection). This is why he says, "and if Christ has not been raised, your faith is futile; you are still in your sins . . . But now Christ has been

---

95. Ibid., 502.

96. Yovel, *Spinoza and Other Heretics*, 2:12–13, notes that Spinoza had three distinctions for defining religion and that he was primarily against organized religion. He says, "Spinoza's ultimate wish, at least in theory, was to have all men attain religion in the philosophical sense" (2:13), referring to the universal moral component composed of loving God and loving one's neighbors. Again, this is not surprising, given that he witnessed the *unloving* actions of his fellow religious authorities and their oppression.

97. Whether or not one believes the gospel of Paul to be true is beyond the point. The point here is simply that Paul believed it to be true and that relaying this was the purpose and occasion of his writing this epistle to the Corinthians.

raised from the dead (εἰ δὲ Χριστὸς οὐκ ἐγήγερται, ματαία ἡ πίστις ὑμῶν, ἔτι ἐστὲ ἐν ταῖς ἁμαρτίαις ὑμῶν . . . Νυνὶ δὲ Χριστὸς ἐγήγερται ἐκ νεκρῶν)" (1 Cor 15:17, 20). Again, as Spinoza contends, whether or not one believes this to be true is not the point; but it is clear that Paul believed it to be true. And if Paul believed it to be true, then his purpose in writing is beyond mere morality, though morality certainly is a result of history.

## Conclusion

In this paper, I have outlined Spinoza's basic beliefs regarding biblical interpretation. Spinoza is known for his skepticism and his naturalistic worldview, which corresponded with—and were most likely caused by—the experiences he had with the religiously orthodox and their hypocrisy. If some of his principles are taken at face value, without understanding the motives and implications behind them, one would possibly consider Spinoza to be an objective interpreter of the text. But we have seen his purpose, as explicitly stated by himself in the preface to his *Theological-Political Treatise* as well as personal correspondence to colleagues. These reveal his underlying motives: (1) to expose the prejudices of the theologians, (2) to realign others' view of him as an atheist (he was a deist but not an atheist), and (3) to defend the freedom to think according to one's own prerogatives. However, it has been seen that his own presuppositions hindered objective biblical interpretation, and consequently, his principles are inconsistent with his application.

Again, I would like to reiterate that given the experiences of religious hypocrisy in his life, it is not surprising that Spinoza went in the direction he did. Though he was a skeptic and naturalist, even the most conservative of theologians, if they have any passions, should be empathetic towards Spinoza.

## Bibliography

Baird, William. *History of New Testament Research*. 2 vols. Minneapolis: Fortress, 1992.

Curley, Edwin. "Notes on a Neglected Masterpiece: Spinoza and the Science of Hermeneutics." In *Spinoza: Critical Assessments of Leading Philosophers*, edited by Genevieve Lloyd, 4 vols., 3:64–97. New York: Routledge, 2001.

Dungan, David Laird. *A History of the Synoptic Problem: The Canon, the Text, the Composition, and the Interpretation of the Gospels*. New York: Doubleday, 1999.

Frampton, Travis L. *Spinoza and the Rise of Historical Criticism of the Bible*. New York: T. & T. Clark, 2006.

Grudem, Wayne A. *The Gift of Prophecy: In the New Testament and Today*. Rev, ed. Wheaton: Crossway, 2000.

Gullan-Whur, Margaret. *Within Reason: The Life of Spinoza*. New York: St. Martin's, 1998.

Hirsch, E. D. *Validity in Meaning*. New Haven, CT: Yale University Press, 1967.

Kasher, Asa, and Shlomo Biderman. "Why Was Baruch de Spinoza Excommunicated?" In *Spinoza: Critical Assessments of Leading Philosophers*, edited by Genevieve Lloyd, 4 vols., 1:51–99. New York: Routledge, 2001.

Keener, Craig S. *Miracles: The Credibility of the New Testament Accounts*. 2 vols. Grand Rapids: Baker Academic, 2011.

Klever, W. N. A. "Spinoza's Life and Works." In *Spinoza: Critical Assessments of Leading Philosophers*, edited by Genevieve Lloyd, 4 vols., 1:3–45. New York: Routledge, 2001.

Louw, J. P., and E. A. Nida. *Greek-English Lexicon of the New Testament: Based on Semantic Domains*. 2nd ed. New York: United Bible Societies, 1989.

Morgan, Michael L., ed. *Spinoza: Complete Works*. Indianapolis, IN: Hackett, 2002.

———. Introduction to "Ethics." In *Spinoza: Complete Works*, 213–15.

———. Introduction to "Political Treatise." In *Spinoza: Complete Works*, 676–78.

———. Introduction to "Principles of Cartesian Philosophy and Metaphysical Thoughts." In *Spinoza: Complete Works*, 108–9.

———. Introduction to "Hebrew Grammar." In *Spinoza: Complete Works*, 584–85.

———. Introduction to "Treatise on the Emendation of the Intellect." In *Spinoza: Complete Works*, 1–2.

———. Introduction to "Short Treatise on God, Man, and His Well-Being." In *Spinoza: Complete Works*, 31–32.

Porter, Stanley E. *Idioms of the Greek New Testament*. 2nd ed. BLG 2. Sheffield: Sheffield Academic, 2004.

———. *Verbal Aspect in the Greek of the New Testament: With Reference to Tense and Mood*. SBG 1. New York: Peter Lang, 1989.

Spinoza, B. *Spinoza: Complete Works*, edited by Michael L. Morgan. Indianapolis, IN: Hackett, 2002.

———. "Letter 30." In *Spinoza: Complete Works*, edited by Morgan, 843–44.

———. "Theological-Political Treatise." In *Spinoza: Complete Works*, edited by Morgan, 383–583.

Strauss, Leo. *Spinoza's Critique of Religion*. Trans. E. M. Sinclair. New York: Schocken, 1965.

Terry, Milton. *Biblical Hermeneutics: A Treatise on the Interpretation of the Old and New Testaments*. Reprint. Grand Rapids: Zondervan, 1974.

Thiselton, Anthony C. *First Epistle to the Corinthians*. NIGTC. Grand Rapids: Eerdmans, 2000.

Tov, Emanuel. *Textual Criticism of the Hebrew Bible*. 3rd ed. Minneapolis: Fortress, 2012.

Walther, Manfred. "Spinoza's Critique of Miracles: A Miracle of Criticism?" In *Spinoza: Critical Assessments of Leading Philosophers*, edited by Genevieve Lloyd, 4 vols., 3:100–12. New York: Routledge, 2001.

Yovel, Yirmiyahu. *Spinoza and Other Heretics*. 2 vols. Princeton: Princeton University Press, 1989.

http://www.mcmaster.ca/mjtm/volume14.htm

Baker, David W. *Isaiah*. ZIBBC. Grand Rapids: Zondervan, 2013. Reviewed by David Fuller.

Bird, Michael F., ed. *Four Views on the Apostle Paul*. Counterpoints: Bible and Theology. Grand Rapids: Zondervan, 2012. Reviewed by Gregory P. Fewster.

Block, Daniel I. *Deuteronomy*. NIV Application Commentary. Grand Rapids: Zondervan, 2012. Reviewed by August H. Konkel.

Bock, Darrell L. *A Theology of Luke and Acts*. Biblical Theology of the New Testament. Grand Rapids: Zondervan, 2012. Reviewed by Byung Pill Choi.

Buchanan, Mark. *Your Church Is Too Safe: Why Following Christ Turns the World Upside-Down*. Grand Rapids: Zondervan, 2012. Reviewed by Mark Willcock.

Burge, Gary M. *Jesus and the Jewish Festivals*. Grand Rapids: Zondervan, 2012. Reviewed by Jonathan Numada.

Daughrity, Dyron D. *Church History: Five Approaches to a Global Discipline*. New York: Peter Lang, 2012. Reviewed by Gordon L. Heath.

Demarest, Bruce, Bradley Nassif, Scott Hahn, Joseph D. Driskill, and Evan Howard. *Four Views on Christian Spirituality*. Grand Rapids: Zondervan, 2012. Reviewed by Lee Beach.

Duvall, J. Scott and Verlyn D. Verbrugge, eds. *Devotions on the Greek New Testament: 52 Reflections to Inspire and Instruct*. Grand Rapids: Zondervan, 2012. Reviewed by David I. Yoon.

Garland, Diana R. *Family Ministry: A Comprehensive Guide*. 2nd ed. Downers Grove IL: IVP Academic, 2012. Reviewed by Kelvin Mutter.

George, Timothy. *Reading Scripture with the Reformers*. Downers Grove, IL: IVP Academic, 2011. Reviewed by Omotayo Fakinlede.

Hilber, John W. *Psalms*. ZIBBC. Grand Rapids: Zondervan, 2013. Reviewed by David Fuller.

Knowles, Michael P. *The Unfolding Mystery of the Divine Name: The God of Sinai in Our Midst*. Downers Grove, IL: InterVarsity, 2012. Reviewed by David G. Barker.

Köstenberger, Andreas J. and David A. Croteau, eds. *Which Bible Translation Should I Use? A Comparison of 4 Major Recent Versions*. Nashville: B&H, 2012. Reviewed by Andrew Rozalowsky.

Kulathungam, Lyman C. D. *The Quest: Christ amidst the Quest*. Eugene, OR: Wipf & Stock, 2012. Reviewed by Lois Dow.

Longman, Tremper, III and David E. Garland, eds. *Numbers–Ruth*. EBC 2. Rev. ed. Grand Rapids: Zondervan, 2012. Reviewed by Gordon Oeste.

Nassif, Bradley. *Bringing Jesus to the Desert: Uncover the Ancient Culture, Discover Hidden Meanings*. Ancient Context, Ancient Faith Series. Grand Rapids: Zondervan, 2012. Reviewed by Christopher W. Crocker.

Plummer, Robert L. and John Mark Terry, eds. *Paul's Missionary Methods: In His Time and Ours*. Downers Grove, IL: InterVarsity, 2012. Reviewed by Lee Beach.

Piper, John. *Love Your Enemies: Jesus' Love Command in the Synoptic Gospels and the Early Church Paraenesis*. Wheaton, IL: Crossway, 2012. Reviewed by Deven K. MacDonald.

Shantz, Douglas H. and Tinu Ruparell, eds. *Christian Thought in the Twenty-first Century: Agenda for the Future*. Eugene, OR: Cascade, 2012. Reviewed by Stan Fowler.

Sweeney, Marvin A. *Tanak: A Theological and Critical Introduction to the Jewish Bible*. Minneapolis, MN: Fortress, 2012. Reviewed by Stephen Dempster.

Sweis, Khaldoun A. and Chad V. Meister, eds. *Christian Apologetics: An Anthology of Primary Sources*. Grand Rapids: Zondervan, 2012. Reviewed by Rick Buck.

Walton, John H. *Genesis*. ZIBBC. Grand Rapids: Zondervan, 2013. Reviewed by David Fuller.

Walton, John H. *Job*. NIVAC. Grand Rapids: Zondervan, 2012. Reviewed by August H. Konkel.

Wong, Priscilla. *Anne Steele and Her Spiritual Vision: Seeing God in the Peaks, Valleys and Plateaus of Life*. Grand Rapids: Reformation Heritage Books, 2012. Reviewed by Christopher W. Crocker.